The Rosemary House Herbs + Spices
PEPPERMINT
THYME
ROSEMARY

*The Rosemary House Dooryard Garden*

*Growing and Using*

# HERBS WITH CONFIDENCE

## RECIPES, GARDENING, CRAFTS

## Bertha Reppert

**Illustrated by Marjorie L. Reppert
and Margaret S. Browne**

Remembrance Press
120 South Market Street
Mechanicsburg, PA 17055

ISBN 0-9617210-0-6

Library of Congress 86-90486

PRINTED IN THE UNITED STATES OF AMERICA

Cover Photography By:
Bryson Leidich, Hbg. PA

First printing 1986.
Second printing 1988.
Third printing 1995.

# *DEDICATION*

This dedication is an adaptation by Margaret S. Browne, taken
from a 1901 herbal *Old Time Gardens* by Alice Morse Earle. It is
one of the author's favorite books. Mrs. Morse subtitled it
*A Book of the Sweet of the Year*.

# *TABLE OF CONTENTS*

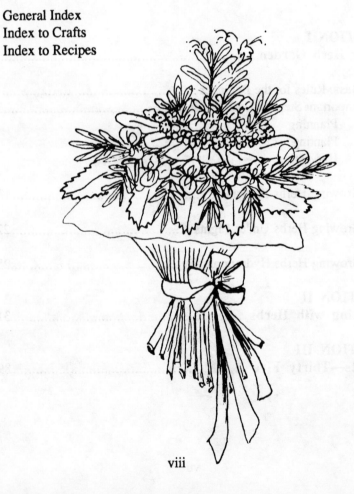

# ACKNOWLEDGMENTS

"And to give thanks is good."

*Swinburne*

My gratitude to all who have contributed to this work is boundless. I am especially grateful for the interest and encouragement of my friends and to the Rosemary House customers who shared their herbal tips with me.

The Penn-Cumberland Garden Club has been holding annual herb teas and programs since 1962. Much of the knowledge, expertise, and recipes developed through this unique series of herbal meetings have been incorporated herein, and I acknowledge with thanks the enthusiastic contribution of this exceptional club.

I especially wish to thank the good cooks who shared their very best tried-and-true family recipes: Gladys Ritter, Mrs. Elmer L. Ritter, Sr., Teresa Kuentz, Hildegard E. Peplau, Mary Smith, Mrs. John Volkl, Roz McMichael, Peggy Waters, Joy Willson, Ginny Fischer, Eve Reppert, Ann Neely, Audrey Stewart, Kathy Horst, Pat Humphries, Martha Deeter Crawford, and Margaret Browne. I would like to extend a special thank you to my daughters Carolynn Sears, Marjorie, Susanna Rebecca, Nancy Reppert, and Friend-Husband Byron, whose special mashed potato filling, now written down, helped win his election as mayor of Mechanisburg.

Although in the field of gardening, indoors or out, I am beholden only to Mother Nature and to the trial-and-error lessons she taught me, I am immensely grateful to all the authors listed in the bibliography, from whom I have gleaned a rich harvest of knowledge of the plants themselves, their uses, ancient and modern, as well as legends and lore. A garland of herbs for each of those who have helped preserve our rightful heritage of herbs by recording this information.

Thanks especially to daughter Marjorie Reppert and to dear friend Margaret Browne, who shared their considerable talents with me in the illustrations. The gardens, herb chart, and frontispiece are Margaret's, while Marjorie did the beautiful drawings from the herbs in my garden.

Finally, a special message of love and gratitude to my "venerable" (her word, never mine!) friend Mrs. R. Bruce Dunlap for introducing me to the virtues of herbs for a lifetime of pleasure. It is her wish and mine that this book will put the same magic in your life.

# INTRODUCTION

As I tend my herb garden, my thoughts frequently wander to "how will I introduce our grandchildren to all the wonders growing around me?" Here I work contentedly, surrounded by plants that are a permanent part of my life in every way just as they have served other households down through the centuries, but how can I be so sure that these timeless herbs will be enjoyed and useful to our space-age generations?

I was introduced to the many joys of herbs years ago by an elderly friend who grew and used them. Trained as a home economist in the early part of the century, she used herbs in her food, in her bath water, in her closets, and in her garden. Herbs, you might say, were her cup of tea, which she was always so eager to share along with her knowledge, her garden, and her experience.

Aha! That's the way to teach herbs. The time-honored precepts of "learn by doing" and "teach by example" would do the trick. All I needed to do to make this my most lasting legacy was write it down along the way.

Learning about herbs by growing and observing them from year to year, then using these little miracles and discovering new uses and rediscovering old ones, has been my greatest joy. Now I am ready to write down what I have learned, passing it along to my family and sharing it with you, dear reader.

Herbs are *the workhorses of the plant kingdom.* I have been gardening all my life, but it is the incredible usefulness of herbs that has lured me ever deeper into their study. Some are grown for fragrance, some are used as seasoning, others are dye or fiber plants, still others are considered insecticides, and all are decorative, fresh or dried. Since the beginning of time, herbs most valued use has been as medicines. We are here today to enjoy 20th century medicines because of the healing virtues of plants.

Today we are no longer totally dependent upon the beneficial powers of herbs. Indeed, they will serve us as well as they ever have in all the ways devised down through the ages, but today we have the leisure and knowledge to enjoy them for pure pleasure.

The word *herb* has had any number of valid definitions. They are herbaceous plants, of course, but sometimes woody. They are the leaves of plants, too, but sometimes it is the oil in the seeds or in the bark that proves most valuable.

Herbs have been counted as useful plants that grow in temperate climates, whereas, spices are those useful plants cultivated in the tropics. Herbs such as saffron and bay and capsicums (peppers), however, frequently overlap such geographical boundaries. They have, however, always been plants with a purpose, something to add much to our lives. As I said before, they are *the workhorses of the plant kingdom*. Learn to use them with confidence.

Herbs cannot be placed in specific categories because some—like camomile, mint, and lavender—have many uses. These three herbs can be medicines, seasonings, and aromatics as well as dyes and insect repellents. Trying to categorize herbs into which will ward off dragons and which will best flavor a chicken can be a tricky business. Most herbs have a multiplicity of uses, and the fun lies in experimenting with their various applications.

Gardening is by far the best way to become familiar enough with herbs to use them with confidence. The year I had my first small herb garden, in 1961, all I did was break off bits and snippets of the fragrant plants, caress the leaves to transfer the oil to my fingers, and breath deeply to enjoy the built-in aroma. The little herbal bunches alerted all my senses as nothing else I've ever grown. Such tiny nosegays were endearing to me. They occupied little vases in my home, went with me everywhere, and sometimes were pressed into the hands of passersby.

Before long, these small bunches of herbs taught me the confidence necessary to use them. They found their way into the cookpot, were dried for potpourris, were experimented with as teas or vinegars, were used as insect repellents in other parts of the garden, and provided gifts for everyone. I was delighted to watch the response to my small gifts. My tokens captured the recipients' attention and hearts like a charm. The magic in herbs truly works!

In order to share my joy with many others, I have written down all the best tricks I know to grow herbs, no matter how small a plot is available, and have given necessary recipes and instructions in order to use the inevitable harvest for creating one's own culinary delights or fragrant crafts. Never again will you be at a loss for a gift whether it be a lovely nosegay, a quart of garden fresh dried parsley, surplus plants from your garden to endow another's plot, or a bowl of sweet-smelling potpourri. Charming, nostalgic, and better than store bought, such herbal remembrances are perfect for everyone on your list. You will use them with confidence.

I guarantee you that inch for inch your herb garden will give you a greater measure of pleasure than you have ever known before and that your personal harvest will be the reputation you gain from knowing and growing and using herbs with confidence. Combine this unexpected prestige with your newfound pleasure, and herbs will continue to reveal their mysteries and become your way of life. In this way, I shall have successfully passed on my personal legacy. My book will be all that I intended—a well-seasoned recipe for happiness.

To grow them is to know them,
To know them is to use them,
To use them is to love them,
And then – happily – Herbs
become your Way of Life.

Bertha Reppert

# YOUR HERB GARDEN

## Basic Rules for the Beginner

To grow an herb garden is to travel back in time, down a long, fragrant path lined with plants of endless usefulness, plants with long histories of service to people.

How to begin this journey? I have a few basic rules for beginning herb gardeners that will help to make it easier. The **first** and most important one is keep the herb garden small. You can easily enlarge the area later, if you wish. In the meantime, even a small patch the size of a dining room table will support a dozen plants, mixed or not, yielding a harvest large enough for an average family. A tub of dirt, a window box, or even a grouping of flowerpots will do for a little garden. Choose a place convenient to your kitchen door or most-used entrance. Putting herbs nearby insures their use.

In reply to the question of what to plant, my **second** bit of advice is start with herbs familiar to you. If these are mint, chives, and parsley, include them in your plans and add, at least, three less familiar herbs, such as basil, thyme, and rosemary.

As with all new fields of endeavor, herb gardening is built on what you know. If you label each herb you plant, you can associate its name with its appearance and its fragrance as you work in your new garden. Before long, you will become so accustomed to these six herbs that you will want to grow six more.

My **third** basic rules is plant your herb garden in a pattern. No matter how small your garden is, it needs a design. Herbs are not flamboyant plants like marigolds or zinnias, screaming, "Here I am! See my beautiful flowers!" They are quiet plants, filled with inner

1

beauty, whose charms must be discovered. They are enhanced by their placement in a garden.

Balance a large plant, such as lavender, with another large plant, such as sage, on the opposite corner. Plant several little clumps of parsley or chives around the edges, and place a large, tubbed plant, a rock, or a statue in the center. Arrange the plants as carefully as you would a vase of flowers, having each plant set off, yet important to the whole. The design will give your garden great distinction, summer and winter.

**Fourth,** keep your herbs clipped. One of the reasons why people are sometimes disillusioned with herb gardening is that herbs quickly become overgrown. Don't be afraid to cut the plants when they look weedy. Maintain the plants at the height or size your garden plot requires. Cut them as often as you like or as needed to sustain the health and vigor of the plant.

Succulent, quick-growing plants such as mint, chives, lemon balm, and comfrey can be cut three to five times or more during a good growing season. Woody lavender and rosemary, however, should be cut less frequently. You will soon learn your herb plants' harvest needs. With very few exceptions, herbs respond well to clipping.

**Fifth,** use your clippings. This rule underscores the fun of herb gardening—having the abundant harvest that even a very small plot will provide. You will be amazed how much you can gather from half a dozen or more plants; you can use this harvest to make the crafts and recipes that appear later in the book.

**Sixth** and finally, *give your plot its proper name* . Always call it "my herb garden," even if it is only a small window box. With its variety of foliage, its subtle coloration, delightful fragrance, and wide usefulness, I know that it will give you great joy.

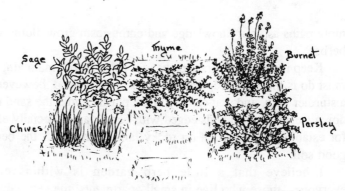

Beginner's Garden

## Planning

Begin by listing the herbs you would most like to grow. Check each one against the list of herbs in the back of this book and note their size, color, use, and any other characteristic of interest to you. If your garden will be shaded, include only shade-tolerant herbs, such as angelica, elecampane, mints, lemon balm, sweet cicely, primrose, flowering tobacco, bee balm, aconite, and sweet woodruff. Experiment with others, of course.

Once your list is complete, you can start "doodling" garden plans on a pad of paper, moving lavender here and parsley there with a whisk of your pencil. This is so much easier than planting and replanting in the garden. Remember that design is vital to the picture you are creating. Balance plants by size, plan contrasting coloration, and add some focus such as a sundial, weathered wood, or a large urn containing mint. Plant tall herbs in the background, of course. Follow this procedure until your garden design pleases you, and you have placed as many of your chosen herbs as possible.

A six-by-six foot space in the sun will provide an abundance of herbs "for use and for delight." To give the garden definition, paths may be necessary.

Several small plots carefully defined by paths will provide an overall design summer and winter. The paths also give you easy access to your herbs in all kinds of weather. Tending and harvesting or showing it to friends will be done with ease. Add small plots and more paths as your knowledge and enthusiasm grow along with the herbs.

Keep in mind that grass paths will be easiest to maintain; all you must do is mow and edge them. Bricks laid in sand, however, make a sturdier path, and you can lay black plastic under the sand to keep down weeds. Raised beds edged with boards are especially effective for establishing a garden on rocky land. Simply fill the beds with good soil.

I believe that a little herb garden is within reach of everyone—those who live in small apartments, the very young, the not-so-young, the gardening novice. If space is available, those who start on a small scale may enlarge their gardens later by repeating the original pattern, perhaps with a grass or brick walk between the sections. After adding little plots and dividing paths—*voila!*—a miniature Williamsburg is created.

By all means, follow your own inclination in this matter, devising a form that best suits your home and lifestyle. As John Parkinson said in the sixteenth century, "To prescribe one forme for every man to follow were too great presumption and folly; for every man will please his own fancie."

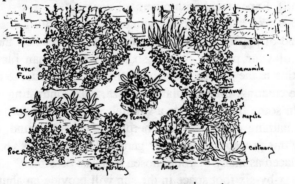

Old Pennsylvania Dutch Herb Garden

## Planting

Since herbs are undemanding plants, good general gardening practices will more than suffice for growing them. Forget about special tools, special fertilizers, or special soil mixes, but do give

4

your herb garden a place in the sun. Although some herbs will tolerate semishade, only a few demand it, and full sun will provide maximum yield. We have two gardens, one in semishade and the other in full sun. Both grow satisfactorily, but the one in full sun grows best.

The ideal site for an herb garden is next to the kitchen door, but among the endless possibilities are the edge of the driveway, the center of an open lawn, or a long, narrow plot against a building.

Good drainage is essential since, except for mint, very few herbs like wet feet. If you suspect a drainage problem in the site you've selected, you can do several things. Either dig the plot deeply and lay a thick bed of cinders or gravel beneath the soil or elevate the bed containing the soil with bricks, boards, or railroad ties. The latter is also a very effective way to set off an herb garden.

Most herbs enjoy alkaline to neutral soil, that is ground that will grow good vegetables but not rhododendron, azalea, or laurel. Lime will help neutralize the soil and should be liberally applied, preferably in the fall or, at least, several months before planting. Even though our soil is naturally rich in limestone, our herb garden benefits from this application of lime every two years. We use ground limestone at the rate of two pounds to every 100 square feet.

The soil itself should be good garden loam, made friable with the addition of compost, peat moss, vermiculite, or sand, whatever you have available to work into the bed. Herbs will settle for clay, but clay is difficult to garden in, and herbs will do better in well-prepared soil, deeply dug, with all the weeds and stones removed.

Save your fertilizer for your roses or tomatoes; most herbs don't need it. Fertilizing leads to rank growth, not the thrifty, compact, strongly aromatic plants you desire. The year we fertilized the herb garden with rabbit manure, we seemed to spend all our time cutting the plants to keep them controlled; they grew with wild abandon, causing a treadmill of harvesting poor-quality plants.

If you are convinced that your soil has no merit, add steamed bone meal or superphosphate, both will aid root growth and produce a better plant as a result. Absolutely avoid nitrogenous fertilizers, especially manures.

Composting and mulching will provide all the soil enrichment most herbs need. We compost weeds, surplus soft cuttings, grass clippings, and all the comfrey we can spare. This rich, fluffy mixture is then returned to the soil every spring as a thick mulch, which improves the tilth of the soil while it helps to keep some of the weeds in check. Mulching also helps the soil retain moisture.

A highly satisfactory mulch, easy to apply (at least three inches every spring), is ground corncobs, obtainable from our local farmers co-op. It has a strange yellow-beige-red color when first applied, but this soon weathers into a pleasing earth tone. Corncobs break down in the soil, encouraging the growth of soil organisms and actually changing difficult clay soil into workable loam.

I also favor comfrey, the gardener's herb. As a mulch and as a compost, comfrey is unsurpassed, Its sturdy roots go deeply into the soil, absorbing minerals vital to healthy plants. A three-year-old comfrey will yield at least five bushels of large, green leaves, richly endowed with these natural fertilizers—all that your herb garden needs to thrive.

We continually harvest a row of comfrey, using this tall plant on the compost pile as an activator or placing it directly around all our plants as a mulch and soil conditioner. Not incidentally, the young, succulent leaves that emerge when comfrey is harvested are edible.

Auxiliary watering in herb gardens is seldom necessary; while less dauntless plants succumb, herbs can survive a rainy season or a drought. No extra watering is one of the reasons why herbs have endeared themselves to me. We do water newly-set plants and plants in pots and window boxes, but we rarely water the herb garden itself, except, perhaps, to wash off foliage prior to harvesting or simply for the joy of smelling the wet, aromatic leaves.

If you have drawn your plans on paper and have prepared your plot, you are ready to plant. Some herbs, such as dill, anise, fennel, and summer savory, are easily grown from seed and, indeed, are best started that way. Plants, of course, make an instant garden and provide a quick harvest of herbs. If a local nursery can't supply the herbs of your choice and you don't wish to risk mail ordering them, by all means, start your own herb plants indoors from seed in early spring. Follow the instructions in the section of this book "Growing

Herbs Indoors," and you will probably start more plants than you have room for—a bonus to share with friends, family, and neighbors.

You may also want to use a cold frame, a simple box-like structure covered with an old window sash and filled with dirt. Not enough can be said in favor of a cold frame for any serious gardener who wishes to start plants from seed or to winter-over uncertain perennials. A cold frame can also provide an extra place where you can grow and harvest such winter-useful herbs as parsley and burnet or where you can pick a bouquet of heartsease, which will bloom by Saint Valentine's Day in a sunny cold frame. Be sure to face your cold frame south to catch maximum sun for heat and light.

Seeds grown directly in the garden, on the other hand, must be planted carefully, only barely covered with soil, then blanketed with a wet cloth or board until germination takes place. The board trick is dandy for starting perennial herbs, especially those that take a long time to germinate or that require fall planting, such as angelica, burnet, wormwood, mole plant, and parsley. Check every now and again to see if the seeds have sprouted, in which case the board should be removed and the herbs permitted to grown.

Most seeds will be up in a week or two, and, weather permitting, they will soon fill your fragrant plot with possibilities. Properly planted herbs will grow like Jack's beanstalk—and grow and grow and grow. Before long, you will be using herbs in ways you never dreamed of before you harvested your own.

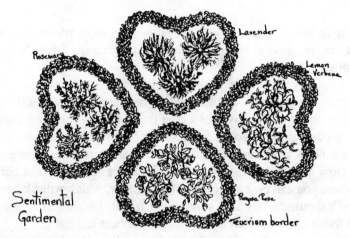

Lavender

Rosemary

Lemon Verbena

Rugosa Rose

Teucrium border

Sentimental Garden

## Harvesting

Cut! Cut! Cut! Keep that little garden clipped and every plant within the bounds allotted to it. Half an hour every day will fly by when you are surrounded by these fragrant herbs, as you work close to the earth, digging and clipping.

A good, sharp pair of flower-cutting shears or a sharp paring knife should accompany you on every trip to the garden. Sometimes, if the garden is large enough and the plantation has grown tremendously, you may want to use a pair of electric hedge shears to make short work of the cutting. If so, lay down a cloth to catch the herbage.

Special cutting instructions for each herb are given in the chapter entitled "The Herbs," but generally cut them as often and as much as you like. Usually a third to a half of the herb can be removed without endangering the plant. Do the cutting on a dry, sunny day before noon. Some herbs, such as comfrey, should be cut within inches of the ground with one plant yielding bushels of useful leaves. Others, such as thyme, need very little pruning. Chives should be cut back right after blooming; and soon they will spring back into the garden picture to be cut again.

Maximum fragrance is present in the leaves just before an herb blooms—the point when commercial harvests are made. Somehow, I cannot quite bring myself to cut all the herbs when they look their best; a blooming herb is at its pinnacle of glory. Therefore, I let some bloom, then I settle for a slightly less fragrance by cutting them back along with the spent blossoms.

In centuries long gone by, when herbs were the only medicines available, it was crucial to their efficacy to pick them at exactly the right point in their growth. Since we are no longer so dependent on herbs for medicines, we can harvest them any time that it suits us, and enjoy the flowers as well.

You will mainly use the herbs you harvest for cooking and crafts, but they may also be used for making teas, cosmetics, repellents, and dyes. Some herbs can be used immediately, such as tarragon, which can be preserved in vinegar. Others must be dried for later use.

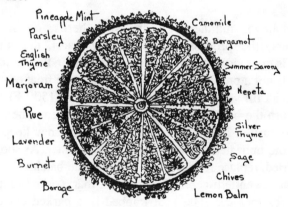

## Preserving the Harvest

Always dry herbs as quickly as possible to preserve color and flavor. One dandy, quick way to dry great quantities of herbs is to scatter the soft tops on old window screens laid flat and supported by bricks.

Other herbs (basil, mints, sage—any leafy herbs) need to be hung in small bunches. We gather them with rubber bands because herbs will contract as the stems dry and shrivel, then we hang the bunches on nails or on an improvised line with clothespins. The settlers always hung them near the fireplace or high in the rafters, wherever heat was trapped. You should also choose a warm, dry, preferably dark place—a garage or an attic.

9

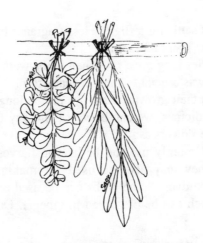

In whatever manner you dry your herbs, on screens or newspapers, the process is hastened by warm, dry air. If the humidity is high, dry the herbs on cookie sheets in the oven. Even if humidity is not a problem, don't deny yourself the treat of having an herbal aroma fill your home. Use very low heat (150° F) for short periods; turn the herbs frequently and remove them when they are completely brittle. If you have a pilot light, you may keep trays of herbs in your unheated oven throughout the summer. As soon as one tray has dried, replace it with a freshly-harvested batch.

Another twentieth-century innovation that works beautifully is drying herbs in a car. The heat trapped in a parked car on a hot summer day will dry herbs quickly; afterward, the car has a heavenly scent.

Using today's kitchen dehydrators, however, is the handiest way to preserve herbs, whether for teas, seasoning, or potpourri. Dried this way, the herbs shrink less and keep more color, fragrance, and flavor.

To use a dehydrator, rinse the leaves of the herbs carefully, and roll them in terry towels to remove excess moisture. Try to keep the leaves as nearly whole as possible so they will retain their flavor. If you want to use the stem and root as well as the leaves (as in the case of comfrey), divide them after rinsing because each portion will dry for a different length of time.

10

Set your dehydrator at a low 95° for leaves or flowers and fill the trays with one layer of herbs. Leaves will take an estimated three to four hours, whereas stems, at 110° F, could take up to nine hours. Keep the temperature low because more heat causes the loss of the oils that give herbs their flavor.

Although using a kitchen dehydrator is the best way to dry parsley (snip them before or after drying, whichever is convenient), using a dehydrator is the worst way to dry lemon verbena. For some mysterious reason, even the slightest heat destroys the lemon verbena's fragrant oils, and the results are disappointing. Air-drying of lemon verbena is still the best procedure.

Colorful petals from red roses, blue larkspur, pink peonies, white mock orange, golden forsythia, and orange marigolds, however, dry beautifully in a dehydrator, making crisp, vivid, full-sized potpourri ingredients. Don't overlook the edible blossoms, either. Violets, strawberry, lilac, honeysuckle, geraniums, redbud, locust, peach, apple, pear, and gay nasturtiums, to name but a few, also dry beautifully by this method. Line up glass jars of the brightly-colored flowers and buds to be used year-round in tossed salads or as garnishes for desserts.

Finally, citrus peels and rose hips from unsprayed old-fashioned roses are also easily dehydrated. Rich in vitamin C, brilliant and flavorful, they are useful as teas and seasonings or in showy potpourris.

If you want to use your microwave oven as a dehydrator, be sure to read the instruction booklet first. Though some ovens are exceedingly fast and convenient, other ovens can be damaged if used incorrectly for this purpose.

After your herbs are dried, by whatever method, strip the stems by drawing them through your fingers. Some people like to hang dried herbs in bags so that the dried leaves may be protected from dust and light, and then crushed by crumpling the bag between the hands. Be sure that all the herbs are "chip dry"—crispy to the senses of touch and sound. When they are crisp, store them in airtight containers. Dark brown jars are splendid because they protect against loss of color, and color is the source of an herb's flavor and fragrance. (Although dried herbs are decorative, they should be stored in the dark, behind cupboard doors.)

Labeling your herbs is important because, once dried, herbs can look much alike. A slip of paper inside or a label on the outside of the container, including the date as well as the name of the herb, will be your insurance against a mistaken identification.

Freezing is the best way to preserve seasonings gathered from the garden, especially chives, which are almost colorless and flavorless when dried. Wash and chop the herb snippets onto a cookie sheet; quick-freeze them and pop them into a labeled freezer container. Herbs may also be frozen in ice cubes and added to soups, stews, and sauces. Herbs such as parsley, chives, or basil may be frozen individually; they may also be combined with thyme, oregano, and rosemary—a kind of frozen *bouquet garni.*

Vinegar is a favorite, old-time preservative for almost any seasoning herb. Easy to use, vinegar will also preserve large quantities faster than any other method—something to consider when your supply of herbs exceeds your need or when your time for preserving them is limited.

To use vinegar as a preservative, stuff a large jar or crock with whichever herb leaves you plan to use. Tarragon is the favorite for vinegars; dill is delicious; burnet is cucumber-flavored; mint is great to have handy; mixed herbs work just fine. Pour near-to-boiling vinegar over the herbs and allow them to steep for at least two weeks. Place the jar in a sunny spot, if possible, and turn occasionally. Strain, bottle, and label the contents for later use.

Seeds such as dill, fennel, caraway, and anise must be dried thoroughly before storing. Add several bay leaves to each of these herbs to discourage insect invaders. Barks and roots must also be cleaned and dried and kept in dry storage. All of these herbs should be housed in opaque jars with tight lids; humidity and light are their enemies.

Preserve every bit of your garden's harvest, especially those herbs such as orange mint, pineapple sage, comfrey, lemon thyme, costmary, rose geranium, woodruff, and sorrel that are not readily available in stores. You'll be glad to have them on your pantry shelves for making the special recipes you will develop along with your garden.

## Growing Herbs Indoors

Windowsill herb gardening has become an American pastime. Even those who aren't smitten with gardening yearn for snippets of practical herbs like parsley, chives, and mints harvested from their own kitchen windows. To tell you that growing herbs indoors is simple would be misleading, but there are ways to garden herbs indoors.

Some important considerations involved in growing herbs indoors are humidity, drainage, sunshine, water, and sometimes fertilization and insect control. All herbs in pots require strong sunshine and cool temperature—conditions that don't often occur together.

Most homes are much too hot and dry for healthy, growing plants. One way to counteract this problem is to group the plants on a tray filled with pebbles. By keeping water in the tray at all times, the water will evaporate and enclose your plants in a little microclimate of high humidity. The water level should never be higher than the pebbles.

Frequent misting is another successful trick for keeping indoor herbs healthy. A fine spray of water works wonders. Spray your herbs as often as possible, and they will reward you with lovely growth. The spray also helps to keep the leaves dust-free.

There are many misters on the market, most of them excellent, but an old window-cleaning sprayer works as well as anything.

Watering, of course, can mean life or death to any houseplant, and especially to herbs. Overwatering and underwatering both cause eventual death to an indoor garden, but overwatering is worse, since its effect—root rot—can't be reversed. Let your finger be your gauge. Poke your finger into the soil; if the soil is wet or even very damp, don't water! It's as simple as that.

I recommend watering herbs in pots from the top, using either rainwater, melted snow, or well or spring water, if available. This is especially important in big city areas where tap water is overchlorinated. Another trick is to fill the watering can and let it set before you water, which causes the chlorine to dissipate into the air. This technique has the added advantage of bringing the water to room temperature—not to mention the advantage of having the water handy when needed.

As for sunshine, if you have a southern exposure in the bathroom, by all means use it, since this also gives you the benefit of humidity. However, if you don't want your sage, thyme and mint in the bathroom—(if you insist on growing them in the kitchen but do not have at least six hours of strong sunlight there), I strongly urge you to invest in a fluorescent plant light. Pots of herbs are a wonderful ornament in a kitchen, but without sufficient light, they will become weak and yellow, then lose their leaves and flavor.

The author's indoor
herb garden,
a sunny south
window

If your herbs are thriving on your windowsill, turn them occasionally to keep them well-rounded, for very strong sunlight will pull all the leaves to one side. Also, pinch the tips as often as possible to keep them from getting leggy; long, gangly stems do not make attractive plants. The pinched parts may be added to your soups, stews, sandwiches, or salads.

Thirty feet of
shelves in the
Reppert
kitchen

If neither strong sun nor artificial light is available, then parsley, thyme, and chives are not for you. Try some of these shade-tolerant herbs: lemon balm, chervil, bay laurel, true myrtle, rue, sweet woodruff, shallots, and well-established mint plants. By all means, experiment with others. And start with plants rather than seeds, since seeds need ideal conditions.

The author's indoor herb garden

A sunny south window is required for basil, thyme, parsley, rosemary, sage, marjoram, burnet, chives, coriander, lavender, dill, catnip, and tarragon. The next best exposure for these herbs is southwest or west. An east window uncovered by curtains or shaded by trees or adjacent buildings will sometimes work; give whatever is available a try.

"Soil," one of my favorite teachers once said, "is the basis of all good gardening." This statement is especially true in the house, where herbs thrive in a standard potting-soil mixture such as one of three equal parts of peat, vermiculite, and soil, to which compost has been added. This combination makes a friable soil, easy to water and keep moist, and one that encourages good root growth and provides the air circulation required by the roots of all potted plants. We frequently purchase a potting soil prepared for houseplants and then mix it with good garden soil and comfrey compost for greater body and extra nutrients. We also add sand or vermiculite for better drainage.

Fortunately, most herbs are disease- and insect-resistant, but if you should happen to have whiteflies, mealybugs, or aphids on your herbs, here are some ways to get rid of them. (Of course, since you will be eating your herb leaves, you won't want to use any of the insecticides having toxic ingredients.) The first thing to try is a simple bath in a sinkful of soapy, warm water—old-fashioned Fels Naptha works best. Wrap plastic around the lower stem of the plant; press it down to cover the soil and to prevent the soil from washing away. Whisk your plant through the water, and rinse it off. Repeat the treatment, if necessary.

Another favorite trick is to soak a cigarette or cigar butt in a pint of water overnight; strain the mixture through cloth and spray the strained portion on the plant, letting some of it drain into the soil where the insects breed. This is remarkably effective; the nicotine, while not harmful to the herb or its uses, does indeed eliminate the pests that bother the plant.

A mild solution of any good liquid houseplant fertilizer once or twice a month will help keep your plants healthy and will give them the stamina needed to grow well indoors in pots. I like a water-soluble fertilizer because it's easy to use, but as an alternative, I sometimes scratch a little bone meal into the top inch of the soil. You might also try a monthly dose of Epsom salts—one tablespoon to a quart of warm water, for sturdy stems, good leaf color, and stronger flavor. Just keep in mind that small amounts of fertilizer, frequently administered, are healthier meals for plants than great doses that may well be more than a little herb can handle.

Success with a few herbs on your windowsill will encourage you to expand your collection by acquiring new plants or by propagating those you already have. Seeds are the most exciting, most convenient, and most economical way to acquire windowsill herbs. Most seeds are easily started by sowing them on vermiculite or milled sphagnum moss, both sterile mediums.

To plant seeds, label the container with the name of the herb and the date and water it thoroughly. After it has drained, place the container in a plastic bag, seal, and set it in the shade. (Fig. 2). When the seeds sprout, remove the plastic and place the seedlings in full sun or very close to fluorescent lamps. This foolproof method will produce herb seedlings faster than any other method.

Figure 2

The marketplace abounds in seed starter kits, mostly plastic greenhouse types, which work well. A plastic bread box, a shoe box, or a large, round hat box can also be recyled into seed starter kits. Tightly lidded, the boxes hold assorted, small, labeled pots of seeds very comfortably, and the shoe boxes can be stacked to save space. Open the lids to check for germination, remove the sprouted herbs and place them in sunlight, then close the boxes on the remaining seeds. At night or when you plan to be away for a few days, even the sprouted herbs can be returned to the box so they don't dry out, which is sure death to seeds and seedlings.

Another thing we have used to start seeds is an old wire lampshade frame (Fig. 3), its silk cover replaced with clear plastic stapled around the wires. This device has covered several pots of seeds or seedlings indoors and small, tender plants outdoors, getting them safely through periods of uncertain spring weather. The lampshade frame fits an old tray, filled with pebbles for good drainage, and make a self-contained, portable unit.

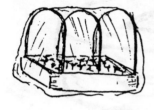

Figures 3 and 4

Another option for growing seeds indoors is a wooden flat filled with vermiculite, then fitted with equidistant wire arches (made from coat hangers) encased in clear plastic to resemble a covered wagon (Fig. 4). This device works extremely well, with one drawback: if you sow more than one kind of seed in any one container, the seeds will germinate unevenly. We fill this flat with smaller, separate flats of seeds, a different kind of seed in each smaller flat. We remove them, one by one, as germination takes place.

One last suggestion—the one that's the most fun of all—is a petri dish. It's perfect for the germination of seeds (Fig. 5), and it's portable besides. Fill the petri dish tightly with well-drained, damp sphagnum moss; sow the seeds, seal with masking tape, and label. Pop the dish in your purse or pocket, or lay it on your desk or on a table where you can inspect it daily. The seeds will seem to explode in your hands. If you carry the petri dish with you, pass it around among your friends while the miracle takes place, and let them share in the excitement.

19

Figure 5

Herbs that we enjoy growing from seeds include burnet, a delicious herb which grows in a tidy, fountain-like clump, dill and basil, which sprout in less than a week; nasturtiums, those plump seeds that even children can handle; and parsley, which is best soaked in warm water before planting, since it has a very hard seed coat that makes germination slow.

For quicker growth, plant cuttings. Start with a four- to six-inch plant. As soon as it roots, you may start snipping—preferably a heel cutting, taken where a side shoot joins the main stem. Scrape the bottom inch of the cutting with a sharp knife, dip it briefly in a commercial rooting power, and plunge the cutting into a small pot of your well-dampened, best soil mixture, pressing it firmly into place.

Next, pop soil and cutting into a plastic bag. Close the bag and keep it away from direct sunlight. When new growth appears, open the bag, remove the young plant, and give it a place in your windowsill herb garden.

Despite the satisfactions of propagating plants from seeds and cuttings, taking plants from the outdoor garden is the fastest way to develop a garden of herbs indoors. Established rosemary, mints, or tarragon plants may be lifted into pots in August, cut back severely if they are very large, and then sunk back into the ground, pot and all, until it is time to bring them in for the winter.

Here's another important tip. Mint and lemon balm, chives, tarragon, and marjoram, like most herbaceous perennials, demand a brief rest because they die back to the ground during winter. Let them rest outside in the pot; bring them indoors around January, when they will erupt into splendid plants, growing rapidly and ready for harvest in a few short weeks. Other plants such as rosemary, bay laurel, pot marjoram, lemon verbena, and scented geraniums should be brought in before the first frost. Ideally all herb plants should be brought indoors and put outdoors on a seasonal cycle, leaving the unnatural environment of the house and enjoying good conditions in the garden during the summer.

I can't say enough in favor of scented geraniums in the indoor herb garden. They are the most amenable of houseplants, coming, as they do, in a splendid variety of forms, colors, and fragrances. You can have an entire herb and spice collection with these geraniums: nutmeg, apple, lemon, rose, ginger, apricot, rose-spice, peppermint, and cinnamon; these are just a few of the many delights to be found in this one group of herbs. Fragrant and edible, these are the easiest of herbs to grow as houseplants, scented geraniums require light feedings and sunshine; they need to be picked and must be allowed to dry out between waterings.

Staging your herbs can bring many hours of pleasure during the winter. Group them together to blend grays and greens, or use them temporarily in an attractive basket as a centerpiece on the dining room table.

Herbs can be placed in tubs, hanging baskets, or, if you have a large windowsill, arranged in matched containers on a tray of pebbles and water. If you plant hanging baskets of herbs, remember that they will dry out much faster than potted plants and may need to be watered each day. Mints, sweet marjoram, prostrate rosemary, pineapple mint, and peppermint geranium make spectacular hanging-basket arrangements. An unused birdcage stand is a most attractive way to display any one of these.

Always remember that proper drainage is absolutely essential for healthy herb plants. Don't use a favorite container unless it has holes in the bottom for drainage. (If you place a potted plant inside a handsome jardiniere or old crock, make sure that water doesn't collect in the bottom. Some pebbles placed in the pot will help, or fill your large containers with small, white, plastic packing peanuts which has recently replaced excelsior. You'll find it never rots and is extremely lightweight, an important consideration for oversized pots.

Sometimes a small label saying "rosemary" or "lavender" means a great deal to observers of your garden. You may know which plants are which, but your friends may not. Remember to use a waterproof pen.

Finally, don't be discouraged if a plant dies. It is simply not the nature of most herbaceous plants to grow indoors for twelve months or more. Enjoy them while you have them, for their uses and fragrance make them special, even for a little while.

If all this sounds like a great deal of work, you'll soon find that, once you start, the routine is pleasant and well worth the effort. Follow these few simple rules of good culture, and the plants will do the rest.

## Growing Herbs Under Lights

If your attempts at growing herbs indoors have been disappointing, the single most likely reason is that you've had insufficient light. Without extraordinarily good window exposure, most indoor herbs will languish.

Fortunately, the use of artificial light—light gardening—makes it possible for everyone to grow healthy herbs indoors. Though our own winter sun isn't strong enough for herbs, a plant light allows me to grow them in our home year-round.

Light gardening is especially adaptable to apartments, where it beautifies and brightens small, dark rooms. There are now so many enthusiasts of this form of indoor gardening that a national organization has been formed: The Indoor Light Gardening Society of America, Inc. (Write to them at Mrs. Virginia F. Elbert, 801 West End Avenue, New York, New York 10025.)

Install these decorative, practical lights inside a tall bookcase, or hang them from a cabinet in the kitchen, where harvests of parsley, sage, rosemary, and thyme make delectable salads. Now you don't need to worry about the sunlight or the width of your windowsills; a plant light will be shining over your herbs, ensuring success in what can otherwise be a risky venture.

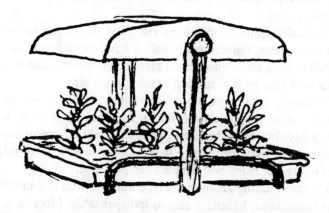

There are a variety of fixtures on the market: small, self-supporting table models, a one-plant "sun-bowl" fixture or floor units with several shelves that will hold dozens of plants. Some of these can be purchased through the mail if they are not available locally.

I've grown kitchen herbs on windowsills and on counter tops under artificial lights, and I find the latter vastly superior. Gardening with lights ranks high in the joys of indoor gardening; this method can work wonders with recalcitrant herbs as well as with one's spirit. When winter snows are piled high and days are short and sometimes dreary, light gardening satisfies all my green-thumbed longings.

My light setup occupies the dark, far corner of a one-window room. The unit is fifty-two inches long and sustains three large trays of healthy plants—dozens of beautiful, scented, green herbs to tend, pick, use, and enjoy. I have added a luxury—a timer, which automatically turns the lights on at 7:00 A.M. and off at 10:00 P.M., giving my herbs fifteen hours of sunlight daily. Let the cold winds blow; the herbs think it is summertime!

Next to providing adequate light, the second greatest difficulty is providing adequate humidity. In the hot, dry atmosphere of the average centrally-heated home. herbs should be kept on waterproof trays of damp vermiculite or stones and sprayed with a fine mist whenever one walks by. A mister filled with water is a necessary tool; keep it at hand. The moisture added to the air will benefit people as well as plants.

To really stimulate plant growth, mist the plants occasionally with soda water. Government studies have proven that the carbon dioxide in soda water encourages plant development. The plants will return your care by replenishing oxygen in the air.

Watering is always a variable factor. During hot summer weather, small plants in little pots sometimes need to be watered twice a day. In winter the same plants in a cool basement may need watering only once or twice a week. Learn to use good judgment; never overwater is the best advice I can give you.

For those daring green-thumbed gardeners who like to start their herbs from seeds, lights are almost indispensable. I like to start my seeds in closed plastic containers placed on top of the light fixture, which radiates just enough heat for germination.

Transfer your small seedlings to pots and elevate them on bricks to positions very close to the lights. To avoid spindly growth, give them the most intense light you can provide. Depending upon the size of each plant, the lights should be twelve to twenty-four inches over the herb. As the young plants develop, lower them gradually into the pans of damp vermiculite, which is easier than raising and lowering the lights. Necessary adjustments in elevation can be made by using inverted flowerpots of various sizes.

I have an artificial light setup in the basement: two plant lights in an ordinary, old fluorescent fixture that I rescued from a trash pile. I use these for a few months during late winter when I have more seedling plants than I've expected. In other homes I have seen basement light setups so extensive that the herbs would have filled a small greenhouse. The advantage of the basement for the herbs is its cool temperature.

It's rather fun to pick tips of marjoram, burnet, chives, tarragon, mints, and basil from these indoor gardens to use as savory seasonings. It's even more fun to pick little fragrant bunches to take to friends. Sprigs of all the herbs, ringed by a few leaves of sweet-scented geranium and tied with gay ribbons, can make the recipient's day.

# Growing Herbs Hydroponically

When indoor gardening beckons, I feel drawn from armchair to window by the promise of green, growing plants. Alas, visions of lush, redolent, green herbs on sunny windowsills rarely come true, especially during short or sunless days.

While growing herbs indoors in pots is not always satisfying, I have had phenomenal success with herbs grown hydroponically. They are healthy, dark green, fast-growing, productive and tasty. You can make a big investment in hydroponic gardening equipment as in everything else; but it is possible to grow herb bouquets through hydroculture with a few, simple household tools. You will need: two pans (plastic wash basins are good) that fit into each other, one slightly deeper than the other; six, six-inch strips of cloth about one inch wide (polyester material won't rot); a good, water-soluble, houseplant fertilizer (Peter's House Plant Special 15-30-15 will do well); vermiculite or any other sterile growing medium; and several sturdy herb plants—parsley, chives, rosemary, sage, and thyme are good to start with.

If you wish to begin with seeds, you will need to germinate them first in separate containers, before transferring the baby seedlings to your hydroculture garden. Seeds tend to rot when exposed to the constant wetness of hydroponics, but cuttings and long shoots develop roots rapidly in the water.

First, drill six, one-half-inch drainage holes in the bottom of the smaller, upper pan. Draw the lengths of fabric through the holes, half in, half out, to act as wicks for carrying the nutrient-growing solution to your herbs. Fill the same pan with a sterile growing medium such as vermiculite, sand, pebbles, gravel, or sphagnum moss. Cover the all-important wicks.

Next, mix two quarts of a well-balanced, houseplant fertilizer solution according to instructions on the label. With your pans nested, pour the solution through the growing medium. The liquid will drip through the holes into the bottom pan. Be sure that only the wicks hang in the liquid, not the bottom of the upper pan. You've now completed the life-support system that will carry food to the roots of the herbs.

Wash all soil from your herb plant roots by gently tapping each root ball and soaking it. This step is important. You might choose to wash the roots in a bucket so as not to clog your drains. Pour the muddy water on your nearest drought-stricken shrub.) As soon as your growing medium is thoroughly dampened, gently tuck the herbs into the upper basin. Because of the intensive feeding process, the herbs can be crowded together to grow twice the number of plants usually possible in the same amount of space.

Now all you need to do for your easy care water garden is to pour fresh fertilizer solution (always mixed with tepid tap water) through the growing medium every week or as often as needed to keep an inch or two in the bottom pan. The fertilizer provides the oxygen essential to plants accustomed to life in soil. The wicks will keep a supply of oxygen flowing to your herbs, causing them to grow at an amazing rate.

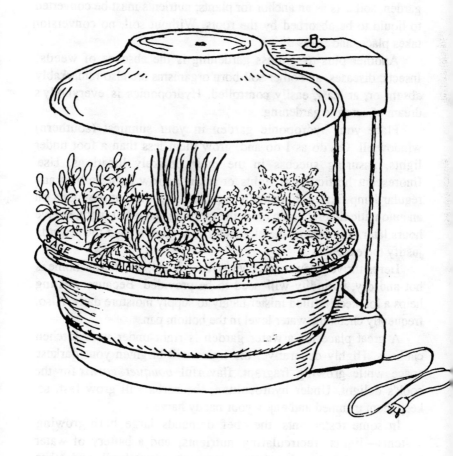

**Growing Herbs Hydroponically Under Lights**

I also advise scratching the surface of the medium occasionally to allow air to reach the roots and to discourage fertilizer salt buildup. In fact, you might poke a dowel through the drainage holes to supply more oxygen to the roots.

Although herbs do not like wet feet in the garden, herbs flourish under water culture simply because no soil is involved. In the garden, soil acts as an anchor for plants; nutrients must be converted to liquid to be absorbed by the roots. Without soil, no conversion takes place, and herbs thrive.

Another plus to soilless gardening is the absence of weeds. Insects, diseases, and other soil-born organisms are also remarkably absent or, at least, easily controlled. Hydroponics is everybody's dream of carefree gardening.

Place your hydroponic garden in your sunniest (southern) windowsill. Or, do as I do and, grow them less than a foot under lights, assuring success in the most unlikely locations. Use fluorescent horticultural lights or insert a grow light bulb in any regular lamp fixture. Eventually, you may want to put the lights on an automatic timer, to turn on in the morning and off at night, twelve hours later. The cost of the electricity is negligible, and the rewards justify the expense.

Herbs thrive in our cool, energy-wise home, but if your home is hot and dry, humidity will need to be provided. Because misting helps a lot, keep a filled mister handy to supply moisture daily. Also, frequently check the water level in the bottom pan.

A great place for a water garden is right under your kitchen cabinets. Highly decorative, the lights will brighten your darkest space while growing fragrant, flavorful *bouquet garnis* for the cook's delight. Under hydroculture, the herbs will grow fast, so keep them trimmed and enjoy your handy harvest.

In some restaurants, the chef demands large herb-growing systems—lights, recirculating nutrients, and a battery of water gardens—to provide the chervil, tarragon, sweet basil, and other fresh herbs for his cuisine. Although this can cost thousands of dollars, my improvised setup comprised of fifty-cent plastic basins and an old, salvaged light fixture is remarkably efficient.

My twelve-inch basin garden supports twice the number of herbs normally grown in a pot of soil that size: rosemary, parsley, winter savory, chives, salad burnet, and dwarf sage. These herbs grow exuberantly and require persistent clipping. One would expect the chive bulbs to rot, but, instead, they produce phenomenally well. My next garden will contain my favorite lemons—lemon balm, lemon thyme, lemon grass, lemon verbena, and lemon-scented geranium, for seasoning, tea, and fragrance.

After a while, you may get so carried away with the easy success of indoor hydroponics that you will want to establish a complete salad patch in your basement. Several kinds of lettuce, spring along with mouth-watering watercress, mint, and dill, will flourish on the shelves of unused closets or in the far corners of a room. No need to brown bag it to the office when it's possible to grow your own low-calorie salad for lunch, complete with Alpine strawberries for dessert.

Later, you can devise automatic water-circulation systems using small aquarium pumps and other such accoutrements—an indoor gardening system that will permit you to cruise The Bahamas while your plants tend to themselves.

# Herb Chart

| | Canapés | Soups | Meats | Fish | Eggs | Chicken | Salad | Vegetable | Breads |
|---|---|---|---|---|---|---|---|---|---|
| **Parsley and Chives** | Dips Garnish Chopped | Browned Garnish Watercress | Chopped Fillings Pies | All seafood | Omelettes Soufflés Sauces Eggs Benedict | Stuffings Chicken corn soup | Fish Egg Tossed Potato | Artichokes Boiled new potatoes Herb butter | Spoonbread Dumplings |
| **Basil** | Crudites mayonnaise Liver paté Tomato slices | Chowders Minestrone Tomato Bean | Stews Roasts Ragouts | Poached Stuffed Aspic Bouillabaisse | Tomato omelette | Casseroles Cacciatore | Cucumbers Tossed green Italian | Carrots Potatoes Ratatouille Especially tomatoes | Luncheon biscuits |
| **Dill** | Anchovies Cottage cheese Pickles | Split pea Tomato Crabmeat Consommé | Veal Pot Roast Smithfield ham Corned beef | Sour cream sauce Halibut Bagged trout | Deviled Soufflé | Filled breasts | Dill weed on cucumbers Potato | Carrots with pineapple Snap beans Avocado | Yeast bread Seed cakes |
| **Mint** | Candied leaves Garnish Cream cheese | Cream of pea Cucumber Potato | Apple stuffing for lamb Sauce for veal or lamb Hamburger | Shrimp dip Poached Trout Boiled | Garnish | | Fruit salads Cucumber Cabbage | Peas Carrots New potatoes | Mint jelly on hot breads |
| **Oregano** | Cheese spreads Little pizzas Antipasto Eggplant | Turtle Onion | Meat sauce for spaghetti Lamb Venison | Tuna fish casserole Baked Swordfish | Scrambled Shirred Spanish omelette | Goose Stuffing Goulash | Tossed green salads | Broccoli Zucchini Tomatoes | On garlic breads Turnovers Sub sandwiches |
| **Rosemary** | Tomato juice | Pea soup Turtle Vegetable purees | With garlic on steak Veal stew | Shrimp Boiled or poached | Deviled | Baked Pheasant Salad | Fruit Tossed | Mashed potatoes Baked eggplant Corn souffle | Meatpie pastry Drop biscuits |
| **Sage** | Cheese spreads Filled celery | Creamed | Sausage Roast beef Veal Pork Pudding | Court bouillon Chowders Eels | Creamed Crepes | Turkey stuffing Sage and oyster dressing Chicken livers | Sparingly (fresh only) | Cabbage Lima beans Peas | Fresh sage butter on hot biscuits |
| **Savory** | In yogurt (with onion) | Bean Clam Tomato | Stews Sausage Rabbit | Chowder | | Chestnut stuffing | Raw vegetable Three bean | All beans Peas Lentils | Whole grain breads French bread |
| **Tarragon** | Vegetable cocktails | Fish soups Mushroom | Rabbit Beef Lamb Steaks | Salmon, hot or cold | Shirred Omelettes | Duck l'orange Roast chicken | Vinegar dressing Green mayonnaise Asparagus | Zucchini Stuffed baked tomatoes Mushrooms | Sandwiches |
| **Thyme** | Paté Cottage cheese Clam dip | Seafood Bouillabaisse | Hamburger All game Swiss steak Lamb | Clam chowder Shrimp All fish | Creole | In stuffing only | Tomato aspic Seafood Pickled beet | Beans Mushrooms Eggplant Onions | Cornbread Cheese sticks |

© Gaynard Sail Designs 1984

30

# COOKING WITH HERBS

*"Better is a dinner of herbs where love is,*
*than a stalled ox and hatred therewith."*

Proverbs 15:17

Any busy person who enjoys cooking as well as eating should learn about the blessings of the simple addition of herbs to food. I can't imagine cooking without herbs.

Because I have limited time for cooking, I depend on the magic of herbs to make cooking easier, and eating more exciting for our family. Any basic family recipe can be enhanced by a pinch of this and a dash of that, and my cookery has been based on this easy-does-it method of seasoning.

Learning to cook with herbs is a requirement for the herb gardener, as well as for the non-gardener who has a flair for cookery. I suggest beginning with familiar herbs—chives, parsley, mint, onions, and celery. Add to this collection herbs you know your family will like. If pizza is a favorite at your house, add the pizza herbs—rosemary, basil, oregano. Also add a few herbs that are not as familiar to you, such as thyme, tarragon, sage, and savory. These herbs, with the addition of garlic, if your family enjoys it, constitute a basic spice cupboard from which many good things are possible. Discard any seasonings your family finds unpalatable and use the remaining herbs with quiet confidence.

Begin with an herb chart or two which you'll find worth countless cookbooks. Pin them inside your cupboard doors or hang, framed, on the kitchen wall. Use the chart in this book to help you develop your own recipes, using moderate amounts of herbs—more

31

of the fresh, if you are lucky enough to have them and less of the more pungent dried, which are always available. Taste as you go along, remembering that it is easier to add herbs than to remove them. You will quickly develop the skill to put excitement and variety in your meals.

In our household we enjoy using almost any of the basic seasoning herbs in moderation; parsley, chives, and basil frequently; but sage and cumin rarely, if ever. A recipe must be adjusted when herbs are added, or culinary efforts are a waste of time. It's interesting, however, that sage goes undetected, even appreciated, in our home when I use it fresh from the garden.

Learn the properties of the most common herbs, certainly of any that you are growing in your garden; then study your family's reaction to the flavors you introduce. Every homemaker's dream is to be comfortable in the kitchen—a dream you'll quickly realize as you practice cooking with herbs. The more experienced you are at cooking with herbs, the more grateful you'll be for the flair it adds to your meals.

Two further words of caution: I rarely use the same herb twice in the same meal, at least not in the same amount. Second, if I make string beans with savory on Tuesday night, I make string beans with rosemary on Wednesday or string beans with dill on Thursday. Further variety can be achieved, of course, by combining two or more herbs into a *bouquet garni*, or herbal bouquet—a blend of several herbs that I'll discuss later in the chapter.

Experimenting with seasonings will teach you the ways of confidence with herbs more quickly than a thousand recipes. You will soon learn to adapt old family favorites as you discover that cooking with herbs is all a matter of taste—taste to be awakened and developed.

32

# Fines Herbes

*Les fines herbes* make delicious additions to cookery as well as useful kitchen gifts for your friends. Many a small cottage herb industry has begun with a special blend of herbs, first tested at home, then given as gifts, and eventually sold as the demand increased.

A typically French seasoning, *fines herbes* is pronounced "fenzerb," with a very soft "r." When Americanized, the term is simply "fine herbs," *Fines herbes* is a blend of usually three or four finely chopped, dried, or fresh herbs.

Finely minced parsley, which blends well with all the other herbs, is always included in a *fines herbes* mixture, usually with chopped chives, and tarragon. (It is perfectly acceptable, however, to use parsley alone when the recipe calls for *fines herbes*. ) Other ingredients for *fines herbes* can be mint, basil, savory, and thyme. Sometimes rosemary, sage, fennel, and oregano, which are considered the more robust herbs, are added in small quantity.

There is no one, definite rule, as some people think, for making *fines herbes*. The ingredients depend on the cook's taste, on what is available, and on the flavor desired in the dish under preparation. The exception is that, in all cases, the herbs must be cut very finely, or they will not be *fines herbes*.

Chervil, the gourmet's parsley, is usually included in this blend because it brings out the flavors of the other herbs. Combined with chives and tarragon, chervil is the peppery, anise-like flavor found in the famous sauce *ravigote* and is an essential ingredient in *bearnaise*.

The *fines herbes* blend I purchased at the famous Culpeper House in London consists of parsley, chives, chervil, and tarragon. This particular mixture is especially good on eggs, salads, and poultry and adds a great deal to tomato juice and fish. Yet another commercial mixture contains chives, marjoram, thyme, and the inevitable parsley, all finely chopped and well blended. This blend is a complement to hamburger, soups, and salads.

To make your own *fines herbes*, choose three or four of your favorite herbs from those mentioned above. Blend your selections in proportions of three, two, and one parts, making sure that one of the herbs dominates. Take the herbs from your garden or use dried ones that you've purchased.

To mince your herbs, bunch several sprigs together and cut them finely, crosswise. Next pile them and mince vigorously with a very sharp knife, regrouping the pile occasionally for further mincing until you truly have *fines herbes*.

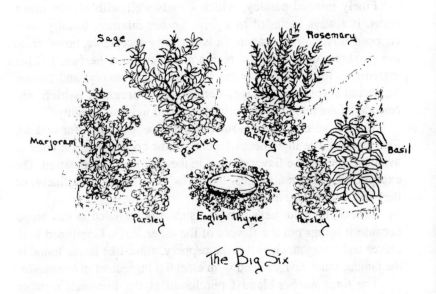

The Big Six

The following recipes will start you on your way.

## Les Fines Herbes

3 ounces parsley
2 ounces chives
1 ounce tarragon
1 ounce chervil

Blend herbs thoroughly. Test on scrambled eggs, adjusting the amounts of the herbs to your own taste.

For gifts, pour the above herbs into pretty, small jars, add a label with hand-written directions for their use, and give them proudly as your own creation.

## Omelette Aux Fines Herbes

3 eggs
Salt and pepper, if desired
1 tablespoon water
1 teaspoon *Les Fines Herbes* (see recipe)

Beat the eggs with a whisk; add remaining ingredients, and cook gently in an 8-inch pan. Fold to serve 2.

## Fines Herbes Bowl

| | |
|---|---|
| 1 | pint sour cream |
| 1/4 | cup chopped parsley |
| 1 | teaspoon salt |
| 2 | tablespoons chopped dill |
| 1/4 | cup chopped chives |
| 1 | green pepper, finely minced |

Mix all ingredients and allow to stand at least an hour before serving as a dip with crisp celery sticks, apple slices, or chips; or serve as a dressing on salads, or baked potatoes, or spread on very dark, thin bread. If available fresh from the garden, burnet is a splendid addition to this recipe.

## Bouquet Garni

Traditionally and literally, a *bouquet garni* is a bouquet of fresh cooking herbs tied with a string into a bunch and added to food. The bunch may be large or small, depending upon the size of the dish in which it is being cooked.

Essential to all good cooking, French or not, the *bouquet garni* is an excellent source of ambrosia in the soups, stews, and sauces that are a part of the everyday cuisine. Although it is always best when made from fresh herbs taken directly from the kitchen garden, fresh herbs aren't always available. If not, substitute dried herbs, tied into a little square of muslin or cheesecloth with a long string attached for easy removal from the cook pot; or to stuff the dried herbs into an empty tea ball and remove it from your dish before serving.

*Bouquet garni* herbs are always added during the last half hour of the cooking process and removed when the best flavor has been imparted. Taste! If you use a generous bunch of herbs, remove it only after five minutes of cooking. Taste! Tasting is the only assurance you have that the flavor is right.

Sometimes *bouquet garni* herbs come already mixed in a bottle and, if you wish, can be added directly to the food. Because they are minced, the purist might call this mixture, *aux fines herbes*.

Cooking herb bouquets may be put together from any assortment of flavors that appeals to you and your family or is available in your garden or at the greengrocer's. Here are some combinations to consider:

1. Basil, chervil, marjoram, chives
2. Parsley, rosemary, thyme, savory
3. Marjoram, thyme, sage, parsley, bay
4. Dill, tarragon, parsley, basil, lovage leaves
5. Summer savory, sage, celery tops, chives
6. Tarragon, chives, oregano, parsley
7. Sage, basil, onion tops, bay
8. Parsley, lemon thyme, rosemary, one red pepper, bay

The directions for these bouquets are general and easy. Tie the herbs together securely with stout string, leaving a long end for retrieval; toss the bunch into your soup or sauce. Be prepared to reap compliments you've never heard before.

# Herb Breads And Butters

One of the easiest ways to use herbs, to capture and utilize their special flavors, is to mix them with sweet butter or margarine. Simply mix one heaping tablespoon of the fresh, minced herbs (or 1/2 teaspoon of the dried) with a quarter pound of butter or margarine. Let the mixture stand overnight to blend the flavors, and the herb butter will be ready to use on toast and hot biscuits or for frying an egg. Refrigerated in a tightly-covered jar, the herb butters will keep very well.

### Garlic Butter

| | |
|---|---|
| 1 | clove garlic, mashed |
| 1 | tablespoon parsley, minced |
| 1/2 | teaspoon thyme |
| 1/2 | teaspoon dill |
| 1/2 | teaspoon oregano |
| 1 | teaspoon lemon juice |
| 1/4 | pound butter or margarine |

Soak the dried herbs in lemon juice for a short time before combining the herbs and softened butter.

Any of the *fines herbes* or *bouquet garni* recipes given previously are suitable for herb butters. You can, of course, devise your own recipe, and use herb butters in many ways: to top hamburgers, steaks, or chops before broiling; to rub on roasts, poultry, or fish before roasting; to sauté liver, onions, or vegetables.

# Herb Breads

Everyone enjoys hot breads, especially when they are spread with herb butters. Although ordinary bread is lifted to a high level with such treatment, making a special bread occasionally can be fun. Here are two treasured recipes to add to your collection. Serve with butter, herbed or not.

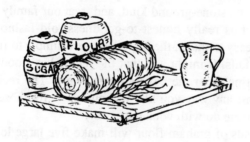

### Rosemary Bread

| | |
|---|---|
| 2 | cups water |
| 1 | cup raisins |
| 2 | teaspoons baking powder |
| 1 | tablespoon crushed rosemary |
| 1/4 | pound butter |
| 2 | cups sugar |
| 2 | eggs |
| 4 | cups flour |
| 1 | teaspoon vanilla |

39

Combine the first four ingredients in a saucepan and bring to a boil. Cook 2 minutes, stirring. Set aside to cool

Meanwhile, cream the butter and sugar in a large bowl; add the eggs and vanilla. Stir in the raisin mixture, alternating with the flour. Pour into six, well-greased soup cans until 2/3 full. Place the cans on a cookie sheet and bake at 350º F for 2 hours, or until done. Cool slightly before removing from the tins.


## Graham Bread


Every now and then I like to buy five pounds of graham (whole wheat) flour, the stone-ground kind, and treat our family and all the neighbors to this really honest-to-goodness, old-fashioned bread. The bread is easy to make, the ingredients are simple to find, and the recipe never fails. (I might add that the recipe has stood the test of time, originating from the covered wagon era. The recipe may be changed almost any way you like without harm, for those were days when cooks made do with what they had.)

Five pounds of graham flour will make five large loaves or ten smaller ones. Although the bread freezes well, we like to give some away; otherwise, we will eat every bit of it!

| | |
|---|---|
| 2 | cups graham flour |
| 1 | cup white flour |
| 2 | cups sour milk* |
| 1/2 | cup granulated sugar |
| 1 | teaspoon baking soda |
| 3 to 4 | tablespoons molasses |
| 1 | teaspoon salt |

Mix all ingredients together in a large bowl. Add any of the following:

Wheat germ
1/2      teaspoon powdered rosemary
1        tablespoon *fines herbes*
1        tablespoon fresh sage, minced
Nuts, dates, candied fruits, or raisins

Pour into a 9x5-inch loaf pan and bake at 375 º F for 1/2 to 3/4 hour.

\* If sour milk is not available, you can make your own. Pour 1 tablespoon vinegar in a measuring cup; add milk to make 1 cup, wait a few minutes for milk to sour.

## Herbed Croutons

By combining cubed, day-old bread with herb butters, the busy cook will have at her fingertips a blend of exciting flavors, which will give many foods a quick lift. Make these seasoned croutons when time permits, store them in a tight canister, and have them ready when needed to toss in a salad, stuff pork chops, add bulk to meat loaf, or top a casserole.

12       slices day-old bread
1/4      pound herbed butter

Cut the bread into cubes, with or without the crusts. Melt the herbed butter in a skillet and brown the croutons slowly and carefully. Spread croutons on a cookie sheet to oven-dry before storing them in a tight tin.

# Herb Salts

When the doctor tells you to "use less salt," remember herbs. Anyone on a low sodium diet can add zest to a bland diet by discovering the secrets of herbs. Eventually, as your taste adjusts, the herbs will do all the work for you that salt had done before. Your dependency on salt will virtually disappear.

All herb salts are made in the same manner. Simply select one of the herb combinations listed below and combine it with an *equal amount of salt* in a blender set at highest speed. Dry the herb salt overnight on a cookie sheet. Store the salt in a labeled canister or salt shaker. Herb combinations can include the following:

1. Celery, basil, thyme, with or without garlic
2. Chervil, chives, tarragon
3. Basil, thyme, rosemary
4. Parsley, sage, celery tops
5. Parsley, chives, oregano
6. Celery seeds, onion flakes, parsley

Use herb salt in soups, salads, dips, and casseroles and on any vegetable or egg dish. For a virtually salt-free diet, reduce the salt and increase the herbs accordingly.

### *Low Sodium Diet Herb Salt*

| | |
|---|---|
| 6 | ounces parsley |
| 2 | ounces lemon thyme |
| 4 | ounces sweet marjoram |
| 2 | ounces savory |

42

|   |   |
|---|---|
| 2 | ounces sweet basil |
| 2 | ounces lemon peel |
| 1 | ounce celery seed |
| 4 | bay leaves |
| 1 | tablespoon salt |

Blend all ingredients in a blender at highest speed until reduced to a fine powder. If fresh herbs are used, dry overnight before storing. This salt will be good on almost everything you cook.

# Herb Jellies

Herb jellies are fun to make, fun to eat, and even more fun to offer as gifts. These sparkling beauties may be served at any meal or with tea.

To make herb jelly, use fresh herbs, whenever available from the garden, by preparing an herb tea in boiling water. Dried herbs, however, are easily substituted. Use one cup of the fresh herb leaves or 1/4 cup of the dried herb for each batch.

### Basic Herb Jelly

| | |
|---|---|
| 1 | cup fresh herb leaves |
| 2 1/2 | cups boiling water |
| 1/4 | cup vinegar |
| 4 1/2 | cups sugar |
| 1/2 | bottle liquid pectin |

Wash the herb leaves and place in a bowl. Pour boiling water over herbs, cover, and steep at least 15 minutes. Strain, retaining 2 cups of the infusion in a saucepan. Add vinegar and sugar and cook over high heat until the sugar is dissolved. Add food coloring, if desired.

When the mixture begins to boil, stir in liquid pectin and bring to a full, rolling boil while stirring constantly. Boil for 1 minute; remove from heat. Skim foam from top and pour jelly into glasses.

Apple juice makes a wonderful base for herb jellies. Using a box of powdered pectin or a bottle of the liquid, follow the above directions or those included with the product. Add a rose geranium leaf to each jelly glass. The leaf will probably wilt, but along the way it gives off a marvelous aroma and flavor missing in ordinary apple jelly.

Other fruit juices may be substituted for the water to make an infusion of greater variety and flavor. Some interesting herb and fruit juice combinations to consider are:

1. Basil and cranberry juice
2. Basil and lemon juice
3. Rosemary and grapefruit juice
4. Sage and cider
5. Thyme and lemon juice
6. Marjoram and grape juice
7. Bay leaf and cider
8. Mint and pineapple juice
9. Parsley and lemon juice
10. Tarragon and lime juice

Developing new combinations is exciting. Experimentation can be great fun, and the results are often extremely good. Write down new recipes as you create them, or you may not be able to duplicate a particularly delicious combination.

Poured into little apothecary jars or brandy snifters, these herb jellies, attractively labeled, sell very well at bake sales and boutiques.

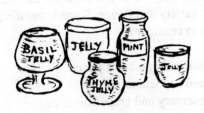

### *Parsley Jelly*

| 3 | cups Prepared Infusion (see recipe below) |
|---|---|
| 4 1/2 | cups sugar |
| 2 | tablespoons lemon juice |
| 1 | box fruit pectin |
| Several drops green food coloring | |

Measure the sugar and set aside. Add lemon juice and pectin to the infusion and mix well. Place over high heat and stir until the mixture comes to a full boil. Stir in the sugar at once. Add enough food coloring to tint; bring back to a full boil. Boil 1 minute, stirring constantly. Remove from heat; skim foam from top and quickly pour into glasses. Seal with paraffin.

**Prepared Infusion:** Wash and chop 2 large bunches of parsley. Place 4 cups of parsley in a bowl and add 3 cups of boiling water. Cover and let stand for 15 minutes; strain, keeping 3 cups of the infusion in a saucepan.

# Salads And Dressings

Mayonnaise was a nuisance to make before the advent of blenders. When you had to add the oil drop by drop while whisking away to prevent separation, the process was tedious. Now, in a minute or two you can have a cupful of good, fresh mayonnaise to use in many recipes. Add the egg yolk without the white if you like a richer dressing.

### Blender Mayonnaise

| | |
|---|---|
| 1 | egg |
| 1 | tablespoon vinegar |
| 1/2 | teaspoon salt (optional) |
| 3/4 | cup vegetable oil |

Put the egg, vinegar, and salt in a blender; add 2 tablespoons oil very slowly while the blender is at its lowest speed. Pour in the remaining oil and continue blending.

## Herbed Mayonnaise

Infinite variations of the above mayonnaise may be made by adding flavorful herbs. Add herbs in the blender, which may turn the mayonnaise green; or make the mayonnaise *aux fines herbes* by hand, and serve it on mixed greens with fish or eggs.

| | |
|---|---|
| 1 | cup Blender Mayonnaise (see recipe) |
| 3 | tablespoons minced chives |
| 6 | sprigs watercress |
| 1 | teaspoon chervil |

## Pink Mayonnaise

| | |
|---|---|
| 1 | cup Blender Mayonnaise (see recipe) |
| 1 | cup chili sauce |
| 1 | teaspoon Worcestershire sauce |
| 1 | tablespoon horseradish |
| 1 | tablespoon dill weed |
| Dash of cayenne | |
| 1 | tablespoon sugar |

Mix all ingredients thoroughly. Serve on shrimp or crab.

## Fruit Dressing

| | |
|---|---|
| 1 | cup Blender Mayonnaise |
| 1 | cup whipped cream |
| 1 | large, dark red rose |

Remove the white, bottom part of the rose petals and discard. Mix the mayonnaise and whipped cream; add the rose petals, cut into very small pieces. Serve on a fruit melange for an elegant luncheon plate.

## Annie's Mustard Dressing

One of the best cooks in my neighborhood contributed the recipe for this tangy and colorful dressing, which is good on potato salad, spinach, lettuce, cabbage, or dandelion greens. The dressing may be frozen and served hot or cold. It is possible, if you like, to substitute 3 tablespoons butter for the bacon.

| | |
|---|---|
| 6 | strips bacon, cut in 1-inch pieces |
| 1 | tablespoon flour |
| 1 | cup sugar |
| 1 | teaspoon ground mustard |
| 1/2 | cup vinegar |
| 6 | tablespoons milk |
| A little pepper | |
| 2 | eggs, well-beaten |

Fry bacon until crisp; set aside. Brown the flour in 6 tablespoons of the remaining bacon fat to make a roux. Mix the sugar, mustard, vinegar, milk, and pepper to add to the roux, cooking until thickened. Remove from heat. With a whisk, slowly add eggs. Return the dressing to the stove until heated, not boiled. Add bacon bits.

## Herbed Finger Salad

The following recipe was entered in a national contest and has stolen the show at every buffet, covered-dish social, or picnic where it has since appeared. This salad is handy to have in the refrigerator, where it keeps well.

Although intended as a finger salad to be cut in small squares, larger squares of the salad may be served on lettuce with mayonnaise. We much prefer it made with fresh herbs, in which case the amounts of oregano, basil, thyme, and rosemary should be doubled.

| | |
|---|---|
| 4 | envelopes unflavored gelatin |
| 3 | packages (3 ounces each) lemon gelatin |
| 4 | cups boiling water |
| 4 | cups celery, finely chopped |
| 1 | green pepper, finely chopped |
| 2 | cups fresh parsley, minced |
| 1 | tablespoon oregano |
| 1 | teaspoon basil |
| 1/2 | teaspoon thyme |
| 1/4 | teaspoon rosemary |
| 1/4 | teaspoon garlic salt |
| 1 | tablespoon vinegar |

13x9-inch pan. Chill until firm. Cut into 1-inch squares to serve. Makes about 100 squares.

### Mimi Ritter's Sauerkraut Salad

As a main dish, relish, vegetable, condiment—there are countless ways to use sauerkraut. No bygone, self-respecting farm family in my part of Pennsylvania considered the harvest complete without crocks full of zesty sauerkraut working away in the cellar. My nose remembers it all too well! Now our twenty-gallon sauerkraut crock, venerated as antique, has found its way to the living room, where it is filled with kindling. How Grandmother would marvel at crocks in the parlor! She would also marvel at this modern version of sauerkraut served as a salad, which keeps well in the refrigerator.

| | |
|---|---|
| 1 | large can of sauerkraut |
| 1 1/4 | cup sugar |
| 1/4 | cup vegetable oil |
| 1/4 | cup vinegar |
| 2 | small pimientos |
| 1 | medium onion, chopped |
| 1 | cup celery, chopped |
| 1 | green pepper, chopped |
| 1 | tablespoon caraway seeds |

51

At least one day before serving, rinse and drain the sauerkraut. Combine sauerkraut with remaining ingredients and refrigerate.

### Marjorie's German Potato Salad

A salad such as this one is a good addition to your cooking repertoire. It is best made ahead and is welcome at picnics, covered-dish socials, or for casual family suppers. Brought back from a memorable trip to Vienna, this German potato salad is a dish with character.

| 6 | old potatoes, cooked in their skins until soft, then chilled about one day |
|---|---|
| 1 | medium onion, chopped |
| 1 | big, red apple, pared and diced |
| 1/2 | medium cucumber, unpeeled and thinly sliced |
| 1/2 | cup parsley, minced |
| Bacon, if desired | |
| 1 | tablespoon salad burnet, minced |

Peel the potatoes and slice them into a large bowl. Add the onion, apple, cucumber, parsley, bacon, and burnet.

**Sauce:**

| | |
|---|---|
| 1 | cup mayonnaise |
| 1 | tablespoon oil |
| 1/4 | cup apple cider vinegar |
| 1 | heaping teaspoon dry mustard |
| 1 | tablespoon sugar |
| 1 | teaspoon salt |
| 1/2 | teaspoon pepper |

Mix all ingredients well and heat, stirring occasionally. Pour over salad mixture.

May be served warm or cold.

## Mother Reppert's Picnic Salad

The following recipe has been in use in our family for many decades and never ceases as a favorite at any outdoor meal, especially during the summer when the vegetables are fresh from the garden. This salad keeps well in a covered jar.

| | |
|---|---|
| 1 | pound cut green beans |
| 1 | pound lima beans |
| 6 | tomatoes, cut into small pieces |
| 1 | onion, finely minced |
| 1/3 | cup vinegar |
| 2/3 | cup sugar |
| 1 | teaspoon savory |
| 1/2 | teaspoon basil |
| Salt and pepper | |

Cook the green and lima beans together until almost done. Add onion and tomatoes. Combine with the remaining ingredients to make a dressing, and pour over the vegetables. Allow this salad to marinate overnight or at least 4 hours before serving.

# Soups

In February 1661, Samuel Pepys wrote in his famous diary, "We did eat some Nettle porridge, which was very good." If you are indisposed toward nettles, try this excellent, hearty soup, which resembles a minestrone but has had its calorie count reduced to a whisper. Theoretically, one burns more calories during digestion of this soup than are consumed by eating it!

### Teresa's Beautiful Soup

| | |
|---|---|
| 4 | stalks celery, diced |
| 2 | onions, minced |
| 1 | quart chicken stock, or 4 cups water combined with 4 teaspoons bouillon |
| 1 | cup wax beans |
| 1 | can cut-up asparagus |
| 1 | large can mushroom pieces |
| 1 | can bean sprouts |
| 1 | package green pea soup mix, hickory smoked |

|      |                                |
|------|--------------------------------|
| 12   | ounces tomato juice            |
| 1/2  | head cabbage, chopped          |
| 1    | zucchini, any size, cubed      |
| 1    | teaspoon garlic powder         |
| 1    | tablespoon summer savory       |
| 1    | tablespoon basil               |
| 1    | teaspoon oregano               |
| 1    | teaspoon freshly ground pepper |

Heat the celery and onions in the chicken stock. Blend the wax beans and asparagus in a blender; add them to the stock. Add all remaining ingredients and simmer 20 to 30 minutes. A thermos of this hearty fare makes a perfect lunch. The soup is even better the second day.


### *Pot-au-Feu*


Thursday is "clean out the refrigerator day" at our house; all leftover dishes—meat, chicken, vegetables, casseroles, cooking broths—are put together into a kind of pot-au-feu. * I cook this version of the French soup-stew with an onion stuck with cloves, celery tops, carrots, cabbage, or turnips—whatever I have—and a sprig of fresh thyme and one whole bay leaf.

If I don't have enough leftover meat, I add half a pound of hamburger to enrich the broth and supply additional protein. In an hour or so I have used up all the odds and ends cluttering the refrigerator, and I have a rich, nutritious, economical meal to serve a hungry family.

Pot-au-feu is traditionally served with the broth first in a soup plate, followed by the meat and vegetables on a dinner plate, but I serve it as a thick soup. Pot-au-feu is always accompanied by a

---

*     Literally "pot-on-the-fire".

crusty loaf of bread cut in thick slices, buttered with herb butter, and heated in foil in the oven for twenty minutes.

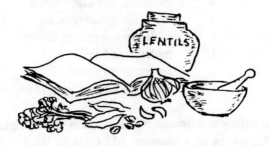

## *Bible Soup*

| | |
|---|---|
| 1/2 | pound lentils |
| 2 | cups boiling water |
| 1 | medium onion, chopped |
| 2 | large cloves garlic, minced |
| 1/4 | teaspoon cumin, if desired |
| 1/4 | teaspoon cardamon |
| 1/4 | teaspoon celery salt |
| 2 | bay leaves |
| 1 | stalk celery |
| 1 | smoked ham hock |
| 4 | cups water |
| 1 | tablespoon parsley, chopped |
| 1 | cup milk |

Remove the boiling water from heat and soak the lentils until the water has cooled. Drain, but do not rinse. In the meantime, brown the onion and garlic. Add the lentils, spices, celery, ham hock, and water; cook for at least two hours. Remove the hock (adding the meat to the lentils) and the bay leaf. Add the parsley and milk just before serving.

# Vegetables

There are so many new ways of preparing and seasoning vegetables that cooking them is becoming more exciting all the time.

The flavor of vegetables can be greatly improved by herbs, particularly when salt and fat are restricted in the diet. If the vegetables cook for only a short time, herbs can be added during the cooking process instead of after. Herb butters, when used, should be added just before serving.

### Byron's Potato Filling

Standard Sunday fare in days long past (when invisible calories didn't count), this very old family recipe is now served by request at all our major family get-togethers. Only the Pennsylvania Dutch could combine potatoes and bread to make such a substantial dish as this, for, as the saying goes, "They know what good is."

Although this family recipe has never been written down before, I have specified the correct amounts of ingredients to serve ten. At our family gatherings, Father presides over the making of this massive dish, which satisfies a Thanksgiving crowd and tastes delicious the second day or after freezing.

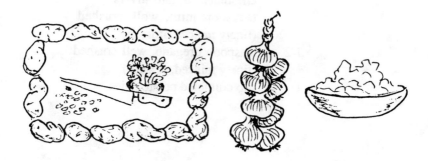

| 1/2 | pound butter or margarine |
| 1/2 | loaf white bread, cubed |
| 1/2 | bunch celery, diced |
| 3 | large onions, sliced |
| 12 | large potatoes, boiled |
| 2 | cups milk |
| 4 | eggs |
| 1 | tablespoon salt |
| 1/2 | cup fresh parsley (if possible), minced |

Melt 1/4 pound butter, each, in two frying pans. In one pan, brown the bread cubes until they are crisped. In the other, stir-fry the celery and onions until softened and translucent. Mash the potatoes, gradually adding the milk, eggs, salt, and parsley. Fold in the cooked celery, onions, and browned bread cubes. Pour into one large ovenware dish or two small ones and bake for 1/2 hour or until the roast is carved.

### Green Pea Casserole

| 1 | large package frozen peas |
| 1 | can cream of mushroom soup, slightly diluted with milk |
| 1 | can water chestnuts or regular chestnuts, cut into slivers |
| 1 | teaspoon mint, well crushed (finely minced, if fresh) |
| 1/2 | teaspoon oregano, well crushed (finely minced, if fresh) |
| 1 | cup crumbled potato chips |

Bring the peas to a boil, but do not cook until done. Drain, and add soup. Add the water chestnuts, sprinkle with mint and oregano, and mix thoroughly. Pour into a greased casserole, top with potato chips, and bake for 30 minutes at 300° F.

## *Herbed Red Beets*

| | |
|---|---|
| 1 | bunch small, new beets (about 1 pound), including roots, peels, and 1 inch of the stems |
| 1 | cup yogurt, warmed |
| 1 | teaspoon fresh parsley, chopped |
| 1 | teaspoon fresh chives, chopped |
| 1 | teaspoon fresh tarragon, chopped |

Boil the red beets for 1/2 hour or until tender. Slip off the skins. Use beets whole, if they are very small; otherwise, slice them. Combine the yogurt and herbs; add the beets. Serve hot or cold.

## *Dilled Pineapple*

Although pineapple is technically not a vegetable, I serve this flavorful fruit as a side dish. Perfect for buffet service, this recipe is best made ahead of time and looks beautiful.

| | |
|---|---|
| 4 | tablespoons sour cream |
| 1/4 | teaspoon salt |
| 1/8 | teaspoon pepper |
| 1 | teaspoon dill weed |

| 1 | No. 2 can pineapple chunks, thoroughly drained |
| 1 | large cucumber, scrubbed and sliced very thin |

Combine the sour cream and seasonings; add the pineapple and cucumber and mix gently. Chill for at least an hour before serving.

### Usha's Indian Rice

This unique recipe takes a bit of doing to assemble the ingredients, especially the herbs and spices, but it will make a spectacular meal for a special occasion. Prepare all the vegetables and measure all the spices ahead of time, to make it easier. Avoid overstirring the rice while it is cooking—once is enough. The dish tends to get mushy if mixed too often.

| 1/3 | cup oil |
| 1/2 | teaspoon whole mustard seed |
| 3 | cloves |
| 5 | cinnamon sticks, 1/2-inch x 1-inch |
| 1/8 | teaspoon ground ginger or 1 tablespoon freshly ground ginger root |

| | |
|---|---|
| 1 | teaspoon sesame seeds |
| 1 | tablespoon salt |
| 3 | cloves garlic |
| 1 | heaping teaspoon ground coriander |
| 3 | cups water |
| 1 | medium potato, diced |
| 1 | medium onion, diced |
| 1 | very small head cauliflower, diced |
| 3/4 | cup yellow corn |
| 3/4 | cup tiny peas |
| 1 or 2 | medium hot peppers |
| 1 1/2 | cups rice, rinsed 3 times |
| 1 | teaspoon turmeric (more if it is pale) |
| 1 | handful blanched nuts (almonds, cashews, peanuts, any alike nuts or combined) |

Using a three-quart pot, heat the oil and mustard seeds until the seeds start to pop. Remove from heat and add all other spices except turmeric; mix well. Add the water, vegetables, and rice, in that order. Stir; then add turmeric. Bring to a boil; turn the heat down to a slow simmer. Cover and cook for 30 to 45 minutes, or until the rice is done. While the rice is cooking, do not stir. Test the rice by pinching a grain between your thumb and finger. If it is not hard in the middle, it is done. Add nuts and serve it forth.

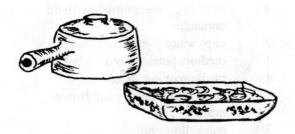

## Baked Tomatoes

When tomatoes are in season, this is one of the many ways we enjoy serving them. Easy to prepare, this dish can be popped into the oven for half an hour or so until the rest of the meal is assembled. Seasonings to add for varying the flavor include oregano, chives, sage, thyme, rosemary, and green peppers.

| | |
|---|---|
| 6 | large tomatoes, sliced 1/2-inch thick |
| 1 | tablespoon sugar |
| 2 | onions, chopped |
| 1 | clove garlic, mashed |
| 1 | tablespoon fresh basil, finely minced |
| 1/4 | cup parsley |
| Salt and pepper | |
| Bread crumbs | |
| Butter or grated cheese | |

Alternate layers of tomatoes with sugar, onions, and seasonings in an ovenproof dish. Cover with bread crumbs and dot with butter or grated cheese. Bake 1/2 hour at 350° F.

62

## Zucchini with Bacon

Zucchini lends itself to herb cookery as no other vegetable ever has. Every one of the culinary herbs can be used with this popular vegetable, alone or in combination, making the versatility of zucchini incomparable.

| | |
|---|---|
| 2 | strips bacon, uncooked |
| 1 | zucchini, cubed |
| 1 | onion, chopped |
| 2 | tomatoes, peeled and chopped |
| 1 | teaspoon sugar |
| Salt and pepper to taste | |
| *Bouquet garni* (basil, oregano, and rosemary are recommended) | |

Cut the bacon in pieces and place in the bottom of a saucepan. Add remaining ingredients. Cover tightly and simmer 10 to 15 minutes, stirring occasionally. Remove *bouquet garni*.

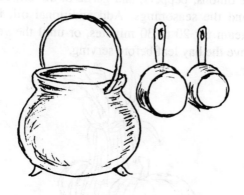

# *Ratatouille*

When the summer vegetable garden is in full swing, a ratatouille is in order. A melange of vegetables simmered with a full complement of herbs, ratatouille is a dish that varies considerably as the harvest progresses.

| | |
|---|---|
| 3 | tablespoons oil |
| 3 | onions, coarsely chopped |
| 2 | green peppers, chopped |
| 3 | clove garlic, finely minced |
| 1 | eggplant, peeled and cubed |
| 2 | zucchini, quartered, seeded, and cut in 1-inch pieces |
| 6 | fresh tomatoes, peeled and cut |
| 1/2 | cup chopped parsley |
| 1/2 | teaspoon thyme |
| 1 | teaspoon basil |
| 1/2 | teaspoon rosemary |
| 1 | teaspoon salt |
| 1 | bay leaf |

Sauté the onions, peppers, and garlic in the oil; add remaining vegetables and the seasonings. Add additional oil, if necessary. Cover and steam for 20 to 30 minutes, or until the vegetables are tender. Remove the bay leaf before serving.

## Pumpkin Chips

The following lemony conserve is adapted from a very old Southern recipe. A good, tart side dish, pumpkin chips go well with almost anything, especially fish or ham. This recipe makes three pints or fills four jelly jars and takes about two hours of cooking time.

| | |
|---|---|
| 1 | firm pumpkin, peeled and sliced |
| | Juice of 12 lemons |
| | Rind of 2 lemons, grated |
| 2 | pounds sugar |
| 1 | root of fresh green ginger |
| 2 | small red peppers |
| 1 | cup small seedless raisins |

Cut pumpkin into chips, about the size of a half dollar, to make two pounds. Combine the chips, lemon juice, lemon rind, and sugar; boil until tender. Remove and save the chips. Add ginger root, peppers, and raisins to the remaining syrup, boil until syrup is thickened. Return the pumpkin chips to the syrup and heat. Pour into jars and seal.

## Eve's Million Dollar Pickles

Nothing gives one a more wonderful sense of accomplishment than putting up pickles for the coming winter. The perfect accompaniment to many meals, homemade pickles also happen to be an unbeatable gift. In the heyday of our vegetable gardening—and before our family was reduced in size—fifty pints of Million Dollar Pickles was my summer's goal. The recipe is aptly named.

| 2 1/2 | quarts water, to which 2/3 cup salt has been added |
| 1 | quart onions, sliced |
| 4 | quarts cucumbers, sliced |
| 2 to 4 | green peppers, sliced |
| 4 | cups sugar |
| 4 | cups vinegar |
| 4 | teaspoons turmeric |
| 4 | teaspoons mustard seed |
| 4 | teaspoons celery seed |
| 2 | pimientos, chopped |

Soak the onions, cucumbers, and peppers in the salt water overnight; drain. Combine all remaining ingredients, bring to a boil, and pour over the drained cucumbers. Simmer 2 minutes. Pour into jars and seal. Makes 4 quarts.

### Quick Pickles

Now that we have reduced our vegetable garden to a fraction of its former size, I resort to easy pickle-making.

| 1/2 | gallon inexpensive dill pickles |
| 2 | large white onions, sliced |

| 2 | cups sugar |
| 1/4 | cup vinegar |
| 1 | teaspoon mustard seed |
| 1 | teaspoon alum |
| 1 | teaspoon celery seed |

Drain the pickles, reserving the juice. Slice alternating layers of pickles and onions into a half-gallon jar or crock. Mix all remaining ingredients in a saucepan, bring to a boil, and pour over the pickles. The pickles should be covered. If necessary, add enough of the original pickle juice to cover them. Refrigerate and eat any time.

# Meats

No matter where you shop, it's almost impossible to find economical meat these days, and many people are refusing to pay the price. Herbs can be the answer to dressing up inexpensive cuts of meat.

If you find yourself resorting to hamburger with increasing frequency, try varying the flavor and presentation. The list of hamburger herbs is almost as long as the alphabet of herbs. Those herbs that enhance ground meat dishes include basil, savory, mint, dill, celery seed, marjoram, parsley, sage, fennel (especially if the meat mixture includes pork), coriander, cumin, curry, and fenugreek. All the onion herbs (chives, shallots, and onions in all forms, including Egyptian) should be freely added unless prohibited by dietary restriction.

Try the above herbs separately if you wish to learn their distinctive flavors; then experiment with different combinations and amounts. The herbs will contribute excitement to an otherwise ordinary dish.

My favorite combination includes liberal amounts of onion, parsley, green pepper, thyme, oregano, and basil. In general, I consider one teaspoon of an herb fresh from the garden equivalent to half that amount of the dried herb.

Mediterranean flavors are achieved by incorporating oregano, basil, rosemary, and garlic in more or less generous quantities. These are the same seasonings (especially the oregano) used to make spaghetti and pizza; don't stint on these herbs if your family enjoys Italian cookery.

## Joy's Fluffy Meat Loaf

One herbal way we practice home economy in cooking is this well-worn recipe for meat loaf. You will find our friend Joy's recipe invaluable. This meat loaf recipe will serve a party of eight, or give a smaller family hearty, delicious leftovers.

| | |
|---|---|
| 1 1/2 | pounds ground meat (beef with pork or veal added) |
| 2 | cups bread crumbs |
| 1 | egg, beaten |
| 1 1/2 | cups milk |
| 4 | tablespoons minced onion |
| 2 | teaspoons salt |
| 1/4 | teaspoon pepper |
| 1/4 | teaspoon dry mustard |
| 1 | tablespoon horseradish |
| 1 | tablespoon catsup |
| 1/2 | teaspoon poultry seasoning |

Mix all ingredients thoroughly and form into one large, or two smaller meat loves. Bake 1 1/2 hours at 350º F for the large one; 1 hour for the smaller loaves.

## Margaret's Mother's Steak

Although this recipe comes from Texas, the seasonings are French, typical of *Haute Provence* . These herbs may be used in the cooking of all kinds of meats, as well as in salad dressings and sauces. The thinly-sliced lemon that disappears in this recipe is the secret to its success. The lemon performs miracles on the meat while blending the seasonings into an indefinable medley of flavors. Your guests will have fun guessing the herbs, and I'll wager that only a few will suggest the lemon, while no one will guess the lavender flowers.

| | |
|---|---|
| 2 1/2 | pounds lean round steak, 2 inches thick |
| 1 | tablespoon oil |
| 1/4 | teaspoon thyme |
| 1/2 | teaspoon fennel leaves or 1/4 teaspoon fennel seeds |
| 1/2 | teaspoon basil |
| 1/2 | teaspoon savory |
| 1/2 | tablespoon lavender flowers |
| 1 | lemon, very thinly sliced |

3 to 5    medium-to-large onions
1         sweet green pepper, chopped
1         6-ounce bottle catsup
Salt and pepper to taste

Brown the meat on both sides in oil and sprinkle with the herbs. Top with the lemon, peel included; smother with half of the onions, a layer of green peppers, and the remaining onions. Pour the catsup over meat and sprinkle with salt and pepper. Bake at 350° F. covered, for 2 hours. Remove the cover and bake another 1/2 hour at 300° F. to create a thick, red gravy. Serve with mashed potatoes.

## Mrs. Volkl's Goulash

Until years after I was married, I didn't know that tomato was used in the making of goulash. Now it seems that more goulash recipes call for tomato than not. My original goulash recipe, using sweet Hungarian paprika, is authentic. It is still a good one to be cherished.

2    pounds round steak, 1 1/2-inches thick
2    large sweet onions
1    tablespoon oil
1    tablespoon flour
3    cups water
3    tablespoons paprika

Cut the steak into cubes and brown with the onions in the oil in an ovenware pan. Add the flour and brown lightly. Mix the water and paprika thoroughly and add to meat. Cover and bake at 350° F. for 2 hours, or until done. Serve on rice or noodles.

### *Sczig Pork Goulash*

A goulash made with tomato has been added to the collection, since this seems to be the most popular way to prepare this famous dish. The cryptic name is taken from the village to which this dish is attributed.

|       |                                  |
|-------|----------------------------------|
| 1/2   | cup flour                        |
| 1/2   | teaspoon pepper                  |
| 1/4   | teaspoon ground ginger           |
| 2     | pounds pork, any cut             |
| 4     | medium-to-large onions           |
| 1     | tablespoon tomato paste          |
| 1     | large potato, peeled and grated  |
| 1     | teaspoon anise or fennel seeds   |
| 1     | can sauerkraut                   |
| 1/2   | teaspoon salt                    |
| 1     | tablespoon sugar                 |
| 1     | tablespoon paprika               |
| 1     | cup sour cream                   |

Combine flour, pepper, and ginger. Cut the pork into 1-inch or smaller cubes and roll in the flour mixture; brown. In another pan, cook the onions until they are softened to a golden yellow; combine with the meat. Add the tomato paste, potato, and seeds; cover. Cook for an hour, or until the meat is done. Add the sauerkraut and cook 1/2 hour longer. Add the seasonings and cook for 15 minutes more. Gently stir in the sour cream until heated. Serve with rice and a salad.

## *Uncle Will's Curry*

Curry powder is a rich mixture of herbs and spices and a wonderfully useful addition to the world of seasonings. Dried and ground, curry powder can contain from five to fifty ingredients, a pinch of which will enliven almost any stew or vegetable dish.

If you are adventurous, you can make your own curry powder, or you can buy any one of a number of commercial preparations. Some powders are so hot you will feel as though you are swallowing a fireball while tears stream down your cheeks. Others are so mild you can season fruit with them, if you wish.

The strength depends entirely upon the amount and potency of the chili used in the mixture. Some of the other herbs and spices that may go into a curry powder are allspice, bay leaves, anise, curry leaves, cumin, dill, fenugreek, fennel, ginger, garlic, mint, mace, turmeric, mustard, peppers, nutmeg, saffron, juniper berries, paprika, and poppy seeds.

Although a curry dish is usually made with lamb or goat, any meat will glory in the flavor combinations of this recipe. Veal cutlet is best.

| | |
|---|---|
| 2 | pounds meat, cut in 1/2-inch cubes |
| 1 | very tart apple, pared and cubed |
| 1 | onion, sliced |

| 1 | banana or plantain, sliced |
| 1 | tablespoon flour |
| 1 | tablespoon medium curry powder |
| 1 | cup bouillon |

Close the meat by browning it in butter. Meanwhile, in another pan, sauté the apple until it is translucent. In yet another pan, cook the onion until tender. Combine the apple and onion with the banana; cook them down to a paste.

Combine the flour, curry powder, and garlic; sprinkle over the browning meat. Add the bouillon and stir to develop the sauce. Add fruit and onion mixture and simmer, covered, until meat is tender. Serve on rice.

# Poultry

The secret of the spectacular success of the Colonel's Kentucky Fried Chicken lies, the company claims, in the combination of ten herbs and spices used to prepare it. You, also, can experiment with preparing chicken with many herbs, alone or in combination, and have something different to serve every time. Choose one or more of the fresh or dried leaves of celery, basil, marjoram, parsley, rosemary, summer savory, sage, paprika. or thyme to give savor to the many dishes prepared from chicken, turkey, or other poultry.

Every spice company markets its own blend called "Poultry Seasoning." A collection of these blends will help you vary the flavor of chicken dishes if you serve chicken frequently; or, you might like to concoct your own blend. Get out the mortar and pestle and start with a clove of garlic, a few leaves of rosemary, some pepper, a dash of nutmeg, 1 teaspoon dill weed, 1/4 teaspoon thyme, 1/2 teaspoon sage, and 1/8 teaspoon paprika, and pulverize the herbs with a vengeance. Add some salt, sprinkle the seasonings on buttered chicken and brown the chicken in a pan. You may find you like this blend much better than the Colonel's!

## Gladys's Matchless Chicken Roll-ups

This easy chicken dish can be accomplished in the time it takes to set the table, steam a vegetable, and toss the salad. Suitable for guests, this dinner entrée for six takes a mere thirty minutes to prepare.

| | |
|---|---|
| 1/2 | teaspoon tarragon |
| 1/4 | teaspoon basil |
| 1 | teaspoon paprika |
| 6 | boned chicken breasts, cut in half |
| 6 | slices of ham, thin |
| 2 | tablespoons butter |
| 1 | can cream of mushroom soup |
| 1/4 | cup dry white wine |

Combine the herbs and sprinkle them over the chicken. Lay the chicken between 2 sheets of waxed paper and flatten with the broad side of a cleaver. Top each piece of chicken with a slice of ham and roll up; secure each roll-up with toothpicks. Brown the roll-ups in butter; stir in the soup and wine. Cover and cook over low heat for 20 minutes, or until done.

## Mary Smith's Escalloped Chicken

This casserole is a favorite chicken recipe for a luncheon. I make the dish the night before and pop it in the oven an hour before serving. It comes out like a soufflé—a gem for the host or hostess who likes to be cool, calm, and collected while greeting guests.

I sometimes vary the recipe by using ham instead of chicken and by serving it for brunch.

| | |
|---|---|
| 8 | slices of crustless bread, buttered |
| 2 | whole, cooked chicken breasts, sliced |
| 8 | slices American cheese |
| 6 | eggs |
| 3 1/2 | cups milk, sprinkled lightly with thyme |
| 4 | rosemary leaves, crushed |
| 1 | tablespoon parsley |
| 1 | cup rolled corn flakes mixed with melted butter |

Grease a 13x9-inch pan and lay the bread in the bottom. Layer the chicken slices on the bread and cover with cheese. In a large bowl, beat the eggs with milk and seasonings; pour over the chicken.

Refrigerate casserole overnight; cover with corn flake crumbs. Bake for 1 hour at 300º F. Serves 12.

## Margaret's Turkey Kiev

This attractive dish makes use of the cut pieces of turkey frequently available at poultry markets. Buy the breast of a bird and have it boned. Serve this turkey roll hot or cold, whether it's Thanksgiving or not.

| | |
|---|---|
| 1 | turkey breast, both sides |
| 2 | tablespoons butter |
| 1 | tablespoon chopped chives |
| 1/2 | teaspoon basil |
| 1/4 | teaspoon marjoram |
| 4 | cups herbed croutons or bread crumbs |
| 1 | cup hot water |
| 1 | onion, chopped |
| 1/4 | teaspoon thyme |
| 1/2 | pound mushrooms, sliced |

Arrange the turkey breasts on a board covered with waxed paper and whack them with a rolling pin until they make a 10x12-inch piece that is not too thin. Spread turkey with butter and herbs. Combine remaining ingredients and spread them on the turkey. Roll up like a jelly roll and tie with string in four places. Lay the roll in a roasting pan dusted with flour; spread the roll with butter, and bake for 2 hours at 375º F. Cover after the first 1/2 hour, or when browned.

# Fish

Fish can be pan-fried, broiled, poached, baked, stuffed, or deep-fried, served elegantly or simply, hot or cold. Fish cookery, indoors or out, is undeniably improved by the use of herbs. The *fines herbes* such as chervil, tarragon, chives, and parsley are a sure choice, but other herbs are willing helpers. Burnet, shallots, thyme, dill, basil, rosemary, fennel, garlic, bay leaf, and even sage are among the herbs to try.

One famous blend of herbs for fish is composed of equal parts of parsley, sweet basil, thyme, fennel seeds, marjoram, and a bit of sage. Devised by a famous chef, this combination will improve even a poor fish, giving it character and distinction. The chef advises that this blend be used sparingly at first, perhaps just 1/8 teaspoon of the blend on each small fish before increasing the amount to satisfy developing.taste. Add salt and pepper as desired.

This particular blend of herbs can be used with any method of preparing fish. Add half a teaspoon to the water, wine, or court bouillon in which you poach your fish. Add 1/4 teaspoon to each pint of fish chowder or oyster stew or add 1/4 teaspoon to a Newburg or Thermidor or any fish with cream sauce.

## Broiled Fish aux Fines Herbes

Our favorite way to prepare a fish fillet is to broil it with an herb butter.

| | |
|---|---|
| 1/2 | cup butter |
| 1 | tablespoon grated lemon rind |
| 1/4 | teaspoon chopped basil |
| 1/4 | teaspoon chervil |
| 1/4 | teaspoon parsley |
| 1/4 | teaspoon chives |
| 1 | pound haddock or flounder fillet |

Blend the butter, lemon rind, and herbs. Spread the herb butter on the fish when it is nearly broiled. Serve the fish sizzling hot, well enhanced by the bubbly, flavorful butter.

## Martha's Fish in a Paper Bag

Calorie counting, economy, high protein, lenten menus, and an angler in the family are only a few of the reasons for exploring fish cookery. If the trout are running, the angler might like to try preparing the catch by using this old Girl Scout trick.

Sprinkle lemon juice, parsley, thyme, and fennel seeds or fennel leaves on the fish you just caught and cleaned. Wrap it in waxed paper, then in very wet newspapers, and finally in a stout, brown paper bag folded over tightly. Cook the bundled fish directly on the hot coals of your campfire for about 15 minutes, until steamed to mouth-watering goodness.

### Trout a La Walden

If you relate completely to nature, and if you will forage unabashedly and, perhaps, barefoot, for herbs, season your catch with zesty wild garlic, peppery watercress, and tart, lemony sour grass before steaming it over an open fire, wrapped in a bag as in the preceding recipe

### Pat's Crunch Tuna Salad

One of the most delightful gifts I have ever received was a pretty basket containing all the main ingredients for Crunch Tuna Salad and the recipe for putting it together. The basket arrived during a busy holiday season when meals were on a catch-as-catch-can basis, and this thoughtful present saved the day. As the attached note read, "It's something a little different for a hurry-up meal on a busy day."

| | |
|---|---|
| 2 | 7-ounce cans tuna, white meat |
| 1 | 8-ounce can water chestnuts, sliced |
| 1/4 | cup diced celery |
| 2 | tablespoons sliced onions |
| 1/2 | cup sour cream |
| 1/4 | cup Italian dressing |

| 1 | tablespoon lemon juice |
| 1/2 | teaspoon salt |
| 1/2 | cup chopped pecans. |

Combine all ingredients and mound on lettuce leaves.

### *Baked Fillet of Sole*

We've already talked about using herbs for special diets; herbs are also valuable in food prepared for the blind. Having little bunches of fresh herbs or mixtures of dried herbs available for pinching and smelling is a most wonderful way to compensate for some of the disadvantage of being unable to see attractively prepared foods. For the baked fillet of sole I would suggest a fresh *bouquet garni* of fennel, dill, tarragon, and a little thyme. Make up two *bouquet garnis*, one to use in the recipe and the other to be held and enjoyed, whether or not it is prepared for the visually handicapped.

| 1 | pound fillet of sole |
| 1 | tablespoon butter |
| 1 | onion, sliced |
| 12 | ripe olives, sliced |
| 12 | mushrooms, sliced |
| 1 | cup white wine |
| 1 | *bouquet garni* |
| 2 | egg yolks |
| 1 | cup cream |

Butter a large glass baking dish. Lay the fish in the baking dish, butter it, and cover with onion, olives, mushrooms, and wine. Add the herbs of your choice, cover with foil, and bake for half an hour or so, until the fish flakes. Remove the *bouquet garni* and transfer the fish to a platter. Thicken the wine sauce by adding the egg yolks and cream; whisk over heat until creamy and thickened. Garnish with fennel or chives.

# Desserts

The fragrance of aromatic herbs can glamorize many ordinary dessert dishes. Frequently, the flavor of the herb reduces the need for sugar in a recipe or satisfies one's appetite for sweets more quickly than sugar. I have assembled a variety of dessert ideas—something for every occasion.

### Fruit Crumble

|     | Apples or strawberries, cut up |
| --- | --- |
| 2 | cups flour |
| 1/2 | cup butter |
| 1/2 | cup sugar |
| 1 | teaspoon crushed coriander seeds, or 3 tablespoons sesame seeds |

Place the fruit in a greased baking dish. Combine the other ingredients until crumbly and sprinkle over the fruit. Bake until the fruit is soft and the crumbs are browned, about 1/2 hour in a moderate oven.

### Holland Cookies

| 1/2 | pound butter |
| --- | --- |
| 1 | cup sugar |
| 1 | egg yolk |
| 2 | cups flour |
| 1/8 | teaspoon cardamom |

81

| 1 | egg white, slightly beaten |
| 1 | cup chopped pecans |
| 2 | ounces poppy seeds, anise seeds, or sesame seeds |

Cream the butter and sugar. Add the egg yolk; add the flour and cardamom. Spread thinly on two ungreased cookie sheets. Coat with egg white and sprinkle with pecans and seeds. Bake 15 minutes at 325º F.

### Strawberry Dessert Salad

| 1 | package (3-ounce) lemon gelatin |
| 1 | package (3-ounce) cherry gelatin |
| 1 1/2 | cup boiling water |
| 18 | ounces crushed pineapple and juice |
| 1 | banana, mashed |
| 1 | 1-pound package frozen strawberries and juice, thawed |
| 1 | cup sour cream |
| 6 | lemon verbena leaves, very finely minced |

Dissolve the gelatins in the boiling water. Add the fruit. Pour half of the mixture into a flat pan and chill until firm. Combine sour cream with herb leaves and spread on top. Pour on remaining gelatin and chill. Garnish with alpine strawberries and lemon verbena tips. Serves 12 to 15.

### *Fruit Compote*

This compote is spectacular enough to be your centerpiece as well as your dessert.

| | |
|---|---|
| 1 | long watermelon |
| 4 | peaches, chopped |
| 1 | unpeeled apple, diced |
| 3 | bananas, sliced |
| | Blueberries |
| | Green grapes |
| | Sweet red cherries, pitted |
| 1 | cantaloupe, scooped into balls |
| 2 | tablespoons lime juice |
| 2 | tablespoons honey |
| 1/2 | teaspoon coriander, ground |
| 1/2 | teaspoon ground nutmeg |
| 1 | cup shredded coconut |
| | Lemon balm and mint leaves |

Cut the top third off the watermelon and flute the edges of the larger piece. Using a melon ball spoon, remove as many perfect balls as possible. Add the remaining fruits to the watermelon, as well as any others that you have available. Combine lime juice, honey, and spices and pour over the fruit. Refrigerate for at least 1 hour.

Garnish the fruit with the lemon balm and mint leaves and ornament the fluted edges of the watermelon bowl with the shredded coconut.

## Mint Parfait

Parfait is so popular and easy, every household should possess the tall, slender glasses traditionally used to serve this elegant yet simple dessert.

| | |
|---|---|
| 1 | quart good vanilla ice cream |
| 1/4 | cup fresh green mint, finely chopped |
| 1 | cup fudge sauce |
| | Whipped cream |
| | Candied violets |

Soften the ice cream in a metal bowl and add the mint. Refreeze until firm. Alternate layers of ice cream and fudge sauce in parfait glasses. Serve with a dollop of whipped cream topped with the purple violet blossoms.

## Meringue Kisses

Meringue kisses are always popular at our garden club's annual herb tea party. They have been served in different guises, by flavoring (vanilla, almond, wintergreen, peppermint, rum, or rosewater) and by decoration (pink candied coriander, yellow candied mimosa, red candied rose petals, green candied mint leaves, or purple candied violets). The possibilities are limitless.

| 4 | egg whites |
|---|---|
| 1/2 | teaspoon cream of tartar |
| 1/4 | teaspoon salt |
| 1 | cup sugar |
| 1 | teaspoon vanilla |
| 1/4 | cup finely chopped mint leaves |

Beat the egg white in a mixer until frothy. Add cream of tartar and salt. Add sugar, one tablespoon at a time, and beat until smooth and all sugar is dissolved. If the sugar is added too quickly, the meringue will not be stiff enough. Gradually add vanilla and mint leaves. Drop onto a cookie sheet covered with greased brown paper. Bake at 200º F or less until firm. Popped into a pre-heated oven turned off and allowed to remain there overnight we call these easy meringues "Forgotten Cookies."

## Poppyseed Cake with Rosewater

Since desserts seem to be served less and less these days, when we do serve one, we like it to be truly gala. This recipe fills that bill; it will produce raves but is deceptively easy to make because it uses several convenience foods. Very rich and crumbly, this cake cannot be served in less than good-sized squares, and must be eaten with a fork.

| 1 | package (18 1/2 ounces) white cake mix |
|---|---|
| 1 | tablespoon butter or margarine, softened |
| 1/3 | cup poppyseed |
| 2 | teaspoons rosewater |
| 1 | 20-ounce can crushed pineapple |

| 1/2 | cup sugar |
| 2 | tablespoons cornstarch |
| The juice of 1/2 lemon | |
| 1 | box 7-minute frosting |

Soak the poppyseeds overnight in water; drain. Prepare the cake mix according to instructions and add butter, poppyseeds, and rosewater. Bake according to directions on cake mix box, for a 13x9-inch cake. Cool in pan 10 minutes before removing to cake rack.

To make the topping, combine pineapple, sugar, cornstarch, and lemon juice and cook in double boiler, stirring until thickened. Cool. Spread topping on cake; frost with 7-minute frosting.

# Beverages

Our children have been very successful at selling lemonade on the sidewalk during local events. Old-fashioned lemonade is always a winner, especially when made with lemon balm and graced with a slice of lemon. Anyone who grows lemon balm probably has plenty that can be put to good purpose in this recipe. Get out your old potato masher and press it into service to make this herby treat.

### Potato Masher Lemonade

| 1 | quart boiling water |
| A | generous handful of lemon balm leaves |
| 1 | quart cold water |
| 2 | lemons, sliced |
| 1 | cup sugar |

Pour the boiling water over the lemon balm leaves. Steep 1/2 hour, then strain, reserving liquid. In the meantime, vigorously mash the sliced lemons and sugar together. Add the cold water and strain into the lemon balm concentrate. Taste and correct sweetening. Serve over ice with sliced lemon and a sprig of lemon balm.

## *Patriot's Punch*

Back in the colonial days, no self-respecting patriot would drink a non-alcoholic punch such as this, but when this recipe was served at a recent reception, 665 cups of the punch were consumed, attesting to its vigor. There was much conversation about the unexpected vitality of the main ingredients, the herbs. There is no reason, however, why you cannot add rum if you wish!

| | |
|---|---|
| 1 | quart water, boiling briskly |
| 5 | tablespoons mint leaves |
| 3 | tablespoons whole rosemary |
| 2 | tablespoons whole sage |
| 1 | cup sugar (optional) |
| 1 | small can frozen lemonade |
| 4 | teaspoons instant tea |
| 2 | gallons cold water |

Pour the boiling water over the herbs and steep for 10 to 20 minutes; strain. To the herb tea add sugar, lemonade, and instant tea, stirring to combine. Pour this concentrate into a punch bowl containing ice and add cold water. Serve with sliced lemons ornamented with whole cloves. Serves 30-40.

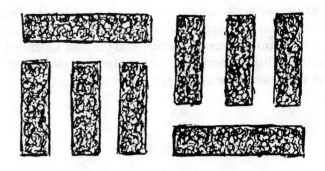

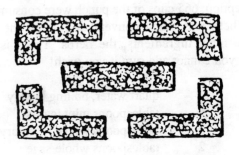

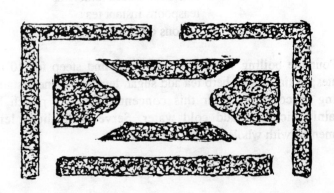

# CRAFTS

## Potpourri (pronounced p͞o - poor - ͞e͞e)

There are as many potpourri recipes as there are people making them. Since the Middle Ages, housewives have captured the fragrance of flowers to put in a pot. Every time someone has varied a recipe according to his or her own disposition, a new potpourri has been born.

Today, grandmother's old-fashioned rose jar is a new idea to many people. The ancient art of potpourri-making has a modern following; it has become a creative, fragrant adventure for today's liberated women.

To make potpourri, begin by gathering rose petals on a pretty day, after the dew has dried, and proceed to dry them in the air or in the oven or by any of the methods described in the section on harvesting (see page 8   ). In the meantime, set about acquiring the herbs, spices, and essential oils necessary for creating your own distinctive aura of fragrance. All aromatic substances can be used in potpourri (the very word *potpourri* has come to mean a collection or mixture of almost anything); the thrill comes in searching out and finding unusual fragrant materials not mentioned here.

Gather many roses, the old-fashioned ones like damask, the *Rosa gallica*, the York and Lancaster rose, *centifolia*, or whatever is available, including modern hybrids. Also collect lavender flowers, elder blossoms, orange blossoms, bergamot heads, golden calendula, pink carnations, dried green ferns, honeysuckle, purple heather, white mock orange, orange safflower, and choice blue delphinium or larkspur florets. Press some pansies and red geraniums to face out from the inside of the potpourri jar. If you like to dry flowers as a hobby and have the necessary equipment, these colorful flowers can be processed in fine white sand, borax, or silica gel. Air drying is most satisfactory, and easiest.

Dried lemon peel, orange peel, lime peel, and other citrus fruit rinds will be valuable additions, for they never lose their essential oil. If you have time, remove as much of the white pith from the rinds as possible; then dry and store the rinds in tightly-covered jars until needed.

Used tea leaves, herb or otherwise, are a grand aromatic ingredient. If you drink tea, you will have a continuing supply of good potpourri materials; or if you are hostess to a large tea party, keep the tea bags and dry them for your collection of fragrances.

Sassafras, cedar wood, sandalwood, rosewood, and all other aromatic woods, chipped fine, as well as pine sawdust and needles, add much to a potpourri. Balsam needles, patchouli leaves, vetiver roots, sweet pipe tobaccos, and rose hips are other fragrant additives.

Herbs from your kitchen garden will add much to your potpourri. Gather all you can of orange mint, lemon balm, lavender, thyme, southernwood, woodruff, and pineapple sage. All the fragrances your herb garden has to offer should be gathered and dried. They will make the potpourri uniquely your own.

To the above herbs you may also add these whole or ground spices from your pantry: nutmeg, vanilla bean, mace, cinnamon, cloves, allspice, cardamom, and juniper.

Some of the oils that will make these ingredients work together are: honeysuckle, bergamot, hyacinth, lavender, rose, lily of the valley, lemon verbena, lime, carnation, violet, rose geranium, mimosa, jasmine, mint, clove, cinnamon, patchouli, lemon, and orange.

In short, do not depend entirely upon your petals for fragrance. Gather and dry them for color and bulk, that's all. I tried many times to make a potpourri just from collected petals, but the more I gathered and dried, the worse they smelled, until I threw the collection away.

Petals alone do not create your fragrant rose jar; the oils and herbs and spices provide the fragrance. Remember this as you gather and dry the colorful bulk of your potpourri. Strange as the method may seem, drying the fragrance out of the rose and then putting it back by using supplemental oil, is the best technique.

The fixative, the ingredient that will hold and blend your fragrances, may be crushed orris root, frankincense, myrrh, gum benzoin, sandalwood, vetiver, tonka beans, or sweet woodruff from your garden.

Once you have assembled all your ingredients—dried petals, citrus peels, tea leaves, fragrant woods, herbs and spices, oil, and a fixative—combine them. Spread plastic, papers or an old sheet on a very large surface. Pour out the colorful petals; add herbs and spices and other fragrances. One or more oils should be added and blended until your potpourri pleases you, but remember that unless the essential oil you are using has been diluted, the fragrance will be intensely concentrated. Add the oil, drop by drop, with caution.

Finally, add the fixative, stirring until you have a uniform mixture. Place the potpourri in a large tin with a tight lid and stir or shake it every day for several weeks. Open the lid occasionally to check the fragrance. If the fragrance is too strong, remove the lid. If the fragrance is not to your liking, add more oil or spices or petals; close the lid and allow the potpourri to mellow for several more weeks.

Now your colorful, fragrant potpourri is ready to be put into attractive jars. You will have plenty for yourself and for your family and friends—some for your favorite Christmas bazaar, too, depending upon how many rose petals you gathered throughout the summer.

Decorate your jars with colorful flowers pressed against the glass, bows tied around the lid, or velvet flowers. Uncover the jar to enjoy your handiwork and close it to reactivate the fragrances.

A very large jarful of potpourri can perfume an entire living room. But if your jar is small, place it by your favorite reading chair, to enjoy while you are sitting there. A huge amount of potpourri can be poured out into a handsome bowl during a party, for all to enjoy. Stir it occasionally to activate its fragrance.

The difference between potpourri and sachet is that potpourri is the mixture used in jars or bowls for fragrance; sachet is the same mixture poured into little sweet bags or flat pillows and placed between linens. Once made, your potpourri can be readily converted into many scented, decorative craft projects.

Potpourri is especially suitable for its sentimental value. A lovely way for a teenage girl to remember her growing-up years is to dry her party corsages, bouquets, boutonnieres, and other floral mementos. This same idea may be applied to someone who has had an illness or accident and has had a great many flowers or get-well bouquets. A new mother also might like to save her flowers as a way of remembering friends and family who sent them.

The idea of collecting and drying flowers for a potpourri or remembrance is especially appropriate for a bride. Flowers from the wedding party, the church, the reception, her home, the showers—all may be gathered, dried, and preserved as potpourri. Such a treasured remembrance will grow more precious through the years.

For those who prefer recipes for making potpourri to directions given above, here are some to try. One last note of caution: Be absolutely sure that everything is "chip dry." The slightest hint of moisture, except the oils, and all is lost.

### *Sentimental Potpourri*

| | |
|---|---|
| 3 | cups dried roses or petals from a special occasion |
| 1 | cup dried herbs (basil, orange mint, lavender) |
| 1/2 | cup rosemary "for remembrance" |

|      |                                      |
|------|--------------------------------------|
| 1/4  | cup ground orris root                |
| 1/4  | cup ground spices (cinnamon, cloves, allspice) |
| 4    | drops rose oil                       |
| 6    | drops jasmine oil                    |
| 2    | drops lemon oil                      |

Mix all ingredients. Store in a tightly-covered container for 6 weeks; stir or shake daily. Transfer to a large glass jar to enjoy.


### *Spring Garden Potpourri*


This recipe makes several small, predominantly yellow potpourris with lemon fragrance. They would be very suitable for a golden wedding anniversary gift.

|      |                                          |
|------|------------------------------------------|
| 2    | cups dried crocus, daffodil, and forsythia flowers |
| 2    | cups dried rose petals, some yellow      |
| 1    | cup dried lemon verbena leaves           |
| 1    | cup dried sweet woodruff                 |
| 1/4  | cup crushed orris                        |
| 1/4  | cup frankincense and myrrh               |
| 1/3  | cup whole cloves                         |
| 12   | drops lemon verbena oil                  |
| 3    | pressed yellow pansies for the side of the jar |

Combine all ingredients, mixing well. Keep covered from 4 to 6 weeks until all fragrances are well blended. Pack gently into pretty jars.

### 1776 Potpourri (Red, White and Blue)

| | |
|---|---|
| 1 | quart red petals (roses, geraniums, bergamot blossoms) |
| 1/2 | quart white blossoms (mock orange, white phlox, pearly everlasting, baby's breath) |
| 1/2 | quart blue flowers (delphinium, hydrangea, larkspur, bachelor's buttons) |
| 2 | ounces crushed orris root |
| 1 | cup lavender |
| 1/4 | cup grains of musk (or a few drops of musk oil) |
| 1/2 | cup lemon verbena leaves |
| 1 | cup mixed spices (cinnamon, cloves, allspice, nutmeg, cardamom) |
| 1/2 | ounce ground tonka beans |
| 1/2 | dram rose oil |
| 2 | drops each of lemon oil, patchouli oil, lavender oil |

Stir together all ingredients. Place in a tightly-lidded container such as a small, clean can, for at least 6 to 8 weeks; stir frequently. Place in pretty jars and tie with red, white, and blue ribbons.

## Eighteenth-Century Moist Potpourri

There are advantages to a moist potpourri; it can be made immediately after harvesting and retains a great deal of fragrance. The disadvantages are its need for more petals and its very dark color. This recipe was adapted from a very old one, which pointed out that the fragrance would last "for your children's children."

Use equal amounts of fresh rose petals of any color, and coarse salt. Press alternate layers of salt and petals into a crock, along with a generous quantity of allspice, cloves, cinnamon, dried lemon verbena leaves, rosemary, patchouli leaves, and mints. Add approximately 1/4 pound gum benzoin, crushed tonka beans, and powdered orris root to act as your fixative. Weight it down. The salt will draw moisture which can be removed as necessary. Empty the crock occasionally, mix the potpourri well, and repack the crock every few days for several weeks—a delightful task. Because no oils are used, the fragrance will be that of your garden. Keep it in an opaque glass jar or an ornate, old ginger jar.

# MORE CRAFTS

These present-day craft items were essential to life in early America. Today we enjoy them for pleasure, to use as special gifts, or to sell as fundraisers.

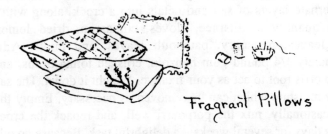

Fragrant Pillows

## *Sleep Pillow*

Cut an 8x12-inch rectangle of firm cotton fabric. Sprinkle 2 cups of hops with alcohol to release the *lupulin* in the hops, which is the soporific. Sew the hops inside the fabric. A delightful gift for a shut-in, the sleep pillow can be pinned to the back of a favorite chair and is said to give relief from insomnia.

## Herbs to Strew

Strewing herbs used to be spread underfoot to keep down the pestilence in the air, "odyferous saveurs," to repel vermin, to cover the dirt, and to fragrance the room. The office of Herb Strewer to the Royal Family, an honorable occupation of centuries past, was only recently discontinued in England by the present Queen Elizabeth.

To sweeten today's trash compactor and garbage disposal or to make vacuum cleaning more pleasant, strew wormwood, rose petals, tansy, mints of all kinds, rue, southernwood, lemon balm, lavender, and rosemary. They may be fresh or dried; or gather together a small, pretty basket of these special strewing herbs, cut into small pieces, to give away. Attach a card explaining their ancient purpose in public buildings, houses, and castles.

## Teasle Wool Teasers

Teasle weed, the fuller's herb, is easily gathered (wear gloves!) along roadsides and fields in the fall of the year, when it is a pernicious weed, but at the same time useful and pretty, too.

To make wool teasers, take teasle heads and clump them together, covering the shortened stems with heavy material, such as denim, tied with ribbons. Use them to remove lint—which is another way of saying to "tease wool," the expression that gives teasle its common name. Hang a resilient teasle weed clump in every closet, and keep them near your sewing equipment. You'll find that teasle niftily picks up dog hair and works well on velvets or upholstered furniture. Store the teasers in clear plastic bags with a label enclosed.

### Excellent Ink

Pokeberries (called *inkberries*) make an acceptable old-fashioned ink when mashed with very little water. Children enjoy making ink. Also try making ink with boiled inky-cap mushrooms, sumac, and the bark of red maples, boiled, or "Elderberries stewed with copperas, vinegar and alum..." says an old formula.

### Fragrant Pillows

Gather lavender, lemon verbena, costmary, all mints, lemon balm, and scented geraniums. Dry the leaves; stuff them into small pillows to scent drawers, closets, chests, and especially linens. You can even sleep upon them.

### Linen Envelope Sachets

These are sachets to place between linens. Make an envelope, approximately 12x18 inches, out of fabric. A beautiful one can be made of satin with an overlay of old-fashioned crocheted doilies held in place with a few stitches. Place crushed potpourri inside, on cotton batting cut to fit. These envelopes are also attractive folded triangularly.

## Sweet Bags

Gather all the fragrant herbs you have, especially lavender and lemon balm, lemon verbena, or lemon geraniums. Add oils, if desired, for greater fragrance. Place a handful of the dried herbs on each 6x6-inch square of cloth (or on an old, pretty hanky); tie with ribbon or lace and store with clothing. Sweet bags are nice in handkerchief or sock drawers, and they never fail to sell well at a ways-and-means table. They are appealing, attractive, sweet-smelling, and useful.

## Sweet Bag Christmas Tree

Use the above sweet bags to decorate a Christmas tree. Tie them on the boughs with red ribbons and give them to your Christmas visitors. Add small pomander balls and cinnamon sticks to the herbs for more fragrance if you wish.

## *Recycled   Greeting   Cards*

Cards are suitable for all occasions, but especially bon voyage because they fit so well in a suitcase. Use any of the cards you have received and found too pretty to discard. Trim the edges with pinking shears so the card will fit in an envelope. Stuff the card with potpourri. Stitch the card shut on the sewing machine, using a zigzag stitch, if you have one. Write your message on the back in prose or poetry. Here's a thinking-of-you message to consider:

> "This sachet card
> Says hello to you;
> Its fragrant wish
> Is special too."

### *Hope  Chest  Sachets*

For the bride, fill a set of white, lace-trimmed satin envelopes of various sizes with lavender or assorted dried herbs and lots of rosemary, the herb sacred to weddings. Lavender is traditionally used to pack away the bridal gown for another generation. Put the sachet between woolens, clothing, and bed sheets, too.

## Grandmother Sachets

When your daughter has a baby, take a memento from her childhood—a bonnet, baby booties, a receiving blanket, or whatever you have saved out of sheer sentiment and stuff it with potpourri to take to her.

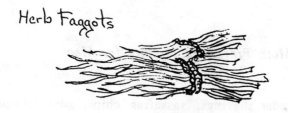

### Herb Fagots

After you finish removing the leaves from bunches of dried herbs, save the stems to use as fragrant fagots to start a cheery fire or to burn as fireplace incense. Lemon verbena, mint, and lavendar are best for this. We tie each bunch with wool or natural twine. To do so, take a 36-inch piece of wool, fold it in half and in half again, and tie it in a simple knot, making many attractive loops as a quick ornamentation. Keep the fagots handy in a fireside basket.

## Tansy Ant Bags

Harvest all the tansy your garden yields, dry it, and put the leaves in little pouch bags made from 4x6-inch pieces of cotton. If hung by the kitchen pipes or wherever the household is plagued by ants, the tansy will repel most ants.

## Moth Prevention Mixture for Men

Use red cedar shavings, sassafras chips, southernwood, patchouli leaves, cloves, and sandalwood, as much as you like, and more of your favorite fragrance. Place this mixture in men's red or blue work handkerchiefs. Fold the handkerchiefs in half and stitch them along the sides. Keep them between sweaters or ski woolens.

## Twentieth Century Herbal Moth Bags

| | |
|---|---|
| 1/2 | cup dried rosemary |
| 1/4 | cup tansy |
| 1/4 | cup southernwood |
| 1/4 | cup thyme |
| 1/4 | cup mint |
| 1/4 | cup pennyroyal |
| 6 | tablespoons ground cloves |
| 6 | tablespoons ground ginger |

Combine the herbs and spices; mix well. Cut 8, 6x6-inch squares of material and 4, 5x5-inch squares of cotton batting. Spread 1/4 of the mixture on each piece of cotton batting and place each square of batting between 2 pieces of material. Stitch all outer seams, pink the edges and decorate with ribbon or lace if you wish. Place these flat, moth-preventing bags between woolens.

## My Favorite Mothballs

> Sandalwood
> Lemon verbena
> Cinnamon
> Patchouli
> Rosemary
> Lavender

Mix thoroughly equal amounts of these herbs, and tie them in squares of calico. Hang the balls in closets or place them in drawers. To use as gifts, be sure to label each one "Herbal Mothball."

## Pomander Balls

Once pomanders were carried to ward off pestilence in the air and to give fragrance. In Europe, the elite used pomander balls made of gold or silver, set with jewels and filled with costly, rare spices and oils. The American colonial housewife made her pomander ball from an orange, when one was available, an apple, or a ball of wax. Wax carried the scent of oils better than any other medium. Old candles can be recycled into spicy pomanders.

To make one for yourself, pick a firm apple or thin-skinned orange and stud it thoroughly with whole cloves. (If you use an apple, be sure it isn't bruised.) The cloves should not be touching. If the skin is hard to penetrate, make preliminary holes with a large needle. After the fruit is covered, roll it in a mixture of 1 part ground orris root, 1 part ground cinnamon, and 1 part ground cloves. If the orange is juicy, so much the better—more of the spices will adhere. Tie with narrow ribbons. Hang the pomander to dry thoroughly and enjoy its spicy aroma. Keep dried pomanders in closets, chests, and drawers to scent your clothing as well as to repel moths. **Note:** They can take up to six weeks to air dry. To speed the process, pomanders can be dried in a slow oven, 150° F for several hours or a day.

Pomanders may also be made from mayapple fruits, quinces, Osage oranges, kumquats, lemons, limes, trifoliate oranges, and the bright, little fruits that develop on Otaheite oranges grown as houseplants in the North.

If you use an apple, be sure it has no bruises. Once studded with cloves, cure it thoroughly in open air. Sometimes people used apple squeezings which are then mixed with cinnamon and cloves and then dried into a hard ball. Thread these balls on yarn before drying, so they may be hung. Leftover bits of wax from candle dippings also served as pomanders. Wax carries the scent of oils better than any other medium. Impregnate the wax with oils such as rose, lavender, orange, or jasmine (spices may also be incorporated). Form into balls and allow the balls to harden.

I have seen pomanders that were almost fifty years old. When yours seem to have lost their fragrance, wash them off and reroll them in the spicy rolling mixture. If they begin to crumble, add them to your next potpourri.

Finally, a word of caution: Pomanders made from fruit must be air-dried before they are packed away in chests or closets. Do not wrap them in tissue or enclose them in plastic; they will mold. If you do not choose to hang them, place them on a screen or in a wicker basket—any location where air can circulate around them for several weeks while they dry completely. In the meantime, keep them near you so you may enjoy their fragrance while they dry. This is the best part of making pomanders.

### Bayberry Candles

Ghostly bayberries are gathered along coastal areas late in the fall. To make these candles, gather a great many bayberries. Boil them in water 10 minutes; cool and collect the wax that hardens on top of the water. Melt the wax over low heat and dip your wick approximately 30 times, or as often as necessary to achieve a candle of desired thickness. The bayberry wax may be extended by the addition of other waxes, such as paraffin, beeswax, or the ends of used candles.

Bayberry candles yield a delicate, spicy odor, especially just after they have been extinguished. This wonderful scent has become the official aroma of a traditional Christmas.

If you make these candles for sale at a boutique or to use as gifts, attach this legend:

> "To learn your luck for the year, they say
> Burn a bayberry dip on Christmas Day'
> If the flame burns bright and the light shines
>      clear,

Good luck will be yours through the coming year."

## *Flat-Iron Waxers*

Even though we no longer use sadirons, today's homemaker will iron more easily by using one of these old-time waxers.

First, prepare bayberry wax as for the candles. Pour the wax on a shallow cookie sheet and cut it into 3-inch squares. Sew each square between two pieces of 4x4-inch cotton fabric. Run your hot iron over the waxer to keep your iron going smoothly.

If bayberry wax is not available, use paraffin. Add to it a few drops of perfume oil, such as bayberry or lemon verbena. The application of perfume oil to the paraffin will make the job of ironing more fragrant!

## *Symbolic  Tussie-Mussies*

A tussie-mussie is a nosegay of fragrant herbs that has a history several centuries long. Once, no well-bred lady would go anywhere without one. Today, as then, you may select tussie-mussie herbs for their fragrance and symbolism. Tie the herbs together with ribbons and a paper lace doily and give them as gifts for the installation of club officers, for anniversaries, bon voyage, and many other special occasions when an ordinary gift won't do. Be sure to attach a note telling what the herbs represent:

| | |
|---|---|
| Rose | for love |
| Rosemary | for remembrance |
| Lavender | for luck |
| Mint | for cheerfulness |
| Sage | for health |
| Thyme | for courage |
| Angelica | for inspiration |
| Burnet | for a merry heart |

## *Money Nosegay*

Herbs can make a gift of money easy and attractive. Pleat the bills and affix an 8-inch length of wire to each one. Incorporate the money on wire stems with a nosegay of fragrant herbs and roses. Tie together with a ribbon, leaving long streamers, and present to the lucky recipient.

## A Bride's Bouquet

A fresh herbal bouquet may be put together according to this old English poem. We also like to press the herbs named in the poem and frame them with a copy of the poem. Sometimes, if there is room, we include the wedding invitation or announcement we received. We substitute scented geranium leaves for the lemon and ginger mentioned.

> "Here's Thyme to give you courage,
> Rosemary for the past.
> Sweet Lavender, a loyal heart,
> Yarrow a love to last.
> Sage for a life that is long and brave,
> Mint to quicken the brain.
> Violets to ward off evil ones,
> Basil to cure the pain.
> And then for fun and fragrance,
> Southernwood will do.
> Rose and Lemon and Ginger
> Mean a sixpence in the shoe."

## Bon Voyage Gift

With any of the symbolic herbs already mentioned, I often gather bay, angelica, St. John'swort, vervain, dill, and other "protective" herbs for a farewell bouquet. I always add mugwort, the traveler's herb, for—so it is said—a leaf placed in the shoe in the morning will allow the wearer to go forty miles before noon without tiring. If I don't have the herbs for a bouquet, I enclose the mugwort, fresh and pressed, in an envelope with a suitable card.

## Protective Doorpiece

For this fall favorite, I use a 1/2-inch dowel cut 15 inches long, with a wire or chain affixed to a screw at the top so that the dowel may be hung on the door. I gather bunches of such protective herbs as mountain ash berries, ivy leaves, and yew, and I tie them together in bunches of short pieces. To these herbs I add wheat for prosperity. Then, beginning at the bottom of the dowel, I tie the clusters of herbs, berries, and wheat firmly to the dowel, overlapping the short bunches as I work toward the top. After adding orange velvet bows in several places, I hang the doorpiece for the fall-through-Thanksgiving season.

## Dieter's Meeting Seeds

In yesteryear, this recipe got one through a long Sunday of prayer and sermons. Combine 2 cups fennel seeds, 1 cup dill, and 1/2 cup caraway seeds. Knot a pinch of the mixed seeds in the corner of a clean handkerchief and nibble them during long committee meetings, at work when the lunch hour is delayed, and in church. The fennel seeds depress the appetite—assuages the "wamblings of the stomach"—and have a delicious licorice flavor. Dill is quieting and soothing.

## *Fido's Herbs*

Fill an old pillow that still has its stuffing with as many of these dried insect-repellent herbs as possible: thyme, bedstraws, pennyroyal, quassia, cedar chips, wormwood, winter savory, elder leaves, and southernwood. (Pennyroyal is the most important.) Present the pillow to your favorite pet.

## *Herbal Bird Cakes with Comfrey*

Save all the kitchen grease you can—bacon fat, beef suet, fat skimmed off soups. Keep the grease in a canister until you have enough to make a good amount of bird cakes. Melt the fats in a large pot and add caraway seeds, nettles, rape seeds, broom-corn seeds, poppy seeds, flax seeds, thistle seeds, canary-seed mixture, crushed corn, eggshells that have been baked in the oven and crushed, hawthorn berries, raisins, and dried comfrey. Mix well, allow the mixture to cool in a large, shallow pan; cut into squares and hang them in a wire mesh bird feeder to attract birds to your garden. The birds will return the favor by also eating thousands of unwelcome insects.

To make the feeder: If your bird cakes are 4x4-inch, cut 1/2-inch wire mesh into 4x8-inch pieces; fold them in half, insert a cake in each, and hang one on a post or tree near your favorite window.

## Herb Wreaths

An herb wreath is the most popular herb craft of all, and easy to do. Collect any round wreath form you can—wire, wicker, straw, sphagnum moss, or coat hangers formed into a circle. To your wreath, using carpet or linen thread (purchased by the spool), tie on your herbal base: goldenrod, all artemisias (especially "Silver King"), mugworts, wormwood, hydrangeas, mints, lemon balm, lavender, ambrosia, or woodruff. Most important, do this while the herb is fresh, as herbs are very brittle when dried. Overlay bunch upon bunch, lay the herb bunches around the wreath form in a continuous circlet of herbs, always wrapping with thread as you go.

Making herb wreaths is a most pleasant, outdoor occupation for a summer or fall day, since you may gather your materials from the herb garden as you need them. Try all the herbs you have in quantity to make this herbal base. Make it full, remembering that the herbs shrink as they dry.

When you ornament the wreath, using the materials you have available, bear in mind that color—harmonizing or contrasting—always makes the most attractive wreath. Attaching clusters of tansy, yarrow, and marjoram flowers to the wreath is one option. "The Fairy" rose, another idea, is one of the loveliest pink additions, especially against a silvery-gray background; picked and placed while fresh, "The Fairy" roses dry to a lovely, softer shade of pink.

All strawflowers, everlastings, grasses, teasles, seedpods, and dried flowers are perfect for this craft. Clusters of spices tied in net bags—cloves, nutmegs, allspice, cinnamon sticks, and such—are fragrant additions. Don't overlook pyracantha, bittersweet, mountain ash berries, and little crabapples, which dry and last a long while.

Bunches of red opal basil, lavender, lemon verbena, sage, lamb's ear, and blue rue are also good herbal additions. They may be dried in sand or silica gel, if you have the time and inclination, or simply poked into the wreath and allowed to dry in place for color and fragrance. Although they lose some of their form this way, they

111

will add much that is distinctively theirs. Top your wreath with a compatibly-colored bow of calico, burlap, or velveteen and hang it proudly on your door.

### Lavender Sachet Wreath

Place a tablespoon of lavender blossoms onto 6x6-inch squares of purple organdy. Gather up the corners of each square, and tie a satin ribbon of a color matching or contrasting with purple, around them. Tie "Silver King" artemisia in a circlet to a 13-inch wicker wreath frame. Cut six 8-inch pieces of ribbon; bring both ends of each ribbon through the wicker, from back to front, and tie in place so that you have six equally spaced ties, grouped at the bottom of the frame. Using these ribbons, affix the lavender sachets, little bunches of grapes, milliner's flowers, or perky bows and make this decoration full and fluffy. Tie a big, loopy bow at the base and a shorter ribbon at the top for hanging. Hang this fragrant wreath in a guest room or bathroom or give it to a convalescent.

### The Victor's Laurels

Ideal for the winner of a tennis match, a political race, or a scholarship, the ancient application of bay laurel comes into its own. Cut a crown (wreath) of sturdy cardboard and cover it with ribbon or material cut on the bias. Staple in place as many dried bay leaves as you wish to use, all of them pointed in one direction. This crown is fun to make and even more fun to present.

## Herb Bouquets

There is no lovelier decoration than herb bouquets for any season of the year, any room, or any occasion. These bouquets are always simple and should be arranged in harmonious containers—something unpretentious in clay or pottery, pewter, unornamented china, or a lined basket. The emphasis is on the form, subtle color, and fragrance of the herbs. Add roses or simple garden flowers, if you like.

First, to create an arrangement, shape a basic triangle or oval out of your most plentiful herb—mint, lemon balm, or boxwood. Use floral foam, vermiculite, or chicken wire in your container to secure the stems. After you have achieved your design, place additional herbs here and there, balancing them against each other and working all the way around the arrangement. The bouquet should be attractive and symmetrical on all viewable sides. Allow for some contrast and fill in with any fragrant herbs you have available. A harmony of foliage always creates the most pleasing bouquet.

This simple bouquet speaks on its own behalf most eloquently; it is quietly endearing—a bouquet different from all others. Place it on your kitchen table or take it to a housebound neighbor.

Dried herbal bouquets are made the same way. Choose your container with care; baskets are excellent since no water is required. Some herbs to gather and dry are hydrangea, goldenrod, teasel heads, angelica seed heads, butterflyweed pods, giant onion tops, lunaria, curved, gray stalks of "Silver King," artemisia, "The Fairy" rose, tansy buttons, yarrow, pearly everlasting, bergamot blooms, perilla seed spikes, and *Artemisia annua* as a fragrant filler.

## Kitchen Spice Ropes

Make six 2x4-inch sacks of gingham and calico. Using all your old bits of leftover wool, braid a thick, 18-inch long rope. Combine 6 crushed nutmegs, 6 broken cinnamon sticks, 6 star anise, 1/8 cup fennel seeds, 1 vanilla bean cut in 1-inch pieces, 1/8 cup allspice, and 1/4 cup cloves. Add an equal quantity of coarse salt, for bulk and to bring out the fragrance. Divide the spices into 6 equal piles and fill the sacks. Use ribbon to tie them to the braided woolen rope, and hang the rope in your kitchen. Crush the sacks occasionally to release more fragrance.

If you prefer, tie 5 small bunches of fragrant herbs from your garden on the rope. Enjoy the aroma while they dry.


## *Sentimental Scenters*

Cut a fat heart pattern from a folded piece of typing paper. Using this as a pattern, cut two hearts of red felt and a smaller heart of cotton batting for each Valentine you plan to make. Pile fragrant potpourri on the cotton; place the cotton on a red heart. Spread glue along the edge of the red heart; lay the other red heart on top and press them together. Presto! You have a fragrant Valentine sachet! Each heart may be ornamented with lace, ribbons, rickrack, little flowers, or sequins, all glued in place. Children can make this handcrafted item very well. It is a good group project.


## *Herb Seed Starter Kits*

Collect all the herb seeds your garden can produce; dry them well and store them, labeled, in little jars. For Christmas gifts, divide the seeds into little envelopes, which you can purchase at a stationery store. Carefully label each packet of seeds and staple it to a sheet of instructions for growing and using the herb seeds inside. Add an appropriate quotation from the Bible or a favorite recipe from an herbal list which uses the herb, as well as the referent that the herb symbolizes. Arrange the seed packets with their legends in gift boxes on which you have glued pressed herb leaves.

## Bible-Leaf Bookmarks

Press the lovely, long leaves of costmary between the pages of a thick telephone book weighted down with a brick. When the leaves are thoroughly pressed, place each leaf on a 2x8-inch piece of colored art paper. An 8-inch length of contrasting ribbon can be glued along the edge for additional color. Write "Costmary Bible-Leaf" along the side and cover with clear contact paper. These items make lovely bookmarks for Bibles or hymnals and perfect gifts for Sunday School attenders of any age. Bible-leaf not only marks the place, it perfumes the book and deters paper-eating insects.

## A Living Herb Wreath

An endearing ornament, a living herb wreath enjoys a special place in our home during Advent and throughout the holiday season. Snippets of fragrant, symbolic herbs and a few gardening and craft supplies are all you need to make this lovely, timely decoration for your home.

To make your living herb wreath, you will need:

| | |
|---|---|
| 1/2 | pound sphagnum moss |
| 1 | 10-inch, 4-wire wreath ring |
| 6 | yards strong carpet thread |
| 1 | 12-inch clear plastic pot saucer (or suitable tray) |
| 2 | cups white pebbles |

An old pencil, sharpened

Rooting powder

2- to 4- dozen 2- to 3-inch herb cuttings such as rosemary, sage, scented geraniums, oregano, rue, thyme, southernwood, mints, lemon balm, Teucrium, bedstraw, woodruff, marjoram, lemon verbena, myrtle, lavender—all kept moist in a saucer of water while you work

Dampen the moss in a bucket of water and squeeze it well before stuffing it into the wire wreath ring. Fill the concave side of the ring to make a full mound. Unless you are planting herbs with roots, wrap with strong thread, going around and around the ring until the dampened moss is securely anchored. If some of the herb plants already have roots, put these herbs in place while stuffing the frame with the moss, carefully securing them as you wrap with thread. It will be easier for you to plant them now than later, and they will be off to a head start.

Next, fill the saucer with pebbles and position the mossed ring in it, mounded side up. All your herb cuttings should be short and sturdy with their bottom leaves removed. Any leaves in the damp moss will only rot, so remove them first.

To plant each cutting, poke a hole in the moss with the pencil, dip each sprig of herb in rooting powder, always shaking off the excess, and poke your cuttings into the holes, one by one. Firm them in place. Arrange them so that the assortment is nicely dispersed throughout the ring.

When finished, mist your living herb wreath and pop it into a large plastic bag (such as a cleaner's bag) for two or three days, or until the herbs stop wilting. Uncover the wreath, and gradually bring it into light and then, because herbs are sunlovers, into your sunniest window, where careful watering and daily misting will help the little herb cuttings take a new lease on life.

Some herbs will perish—don't fret. These can be replaced, or, eventually, the herbs that remain will happily fill the wreath with a network of new, white water roots and fragrant tops, curling in delight around the edges of the saucer. Vigorous herbs that get out of bounds can be pinned with a hairpin or fern pin into the moss, where they will again take root, continuing to fill any empty spaces.

The completed wreath, growing lustily, must be kept damp and exposed to sunlight. Whenever you entertain, the wreath is a fragrant, instant centerpiece surrounding a fat, scented candle or a taper inside a Williamsburg-type glass chimney. Simply by changing the bows or candles, you can make the wreath suitable to all holidays. Your guests will be fascinated by this enchanting herb garden in miniature.

To care for your living herb wreath, mist it daily, water it frequently, and always keep water on the stones, which provide the drainage essential to the herbs' well-being.

Fertilize the wreath with any good houseplant food at least once a month and keep it growing in a sunny windowsill when not being used as a decoration. Cut back extremely long growth to keep it neat (you can toss the culinary herb cuttings into your next salad,) and tuck extra trimmings into the little open spaces to keep your living herb wreath nice and full.

Enjoy the herb wreath on the picnic table during the summer, and bring it back inside for the next holiday season. Your little, circular herb garden should last for at least a year, perhaps more.

## *The Advent Wreath*

Choose a sphagnum moss ring that will fit on a plate or tray, since this wreath must be kept moist. Florists carry the sphagnum rings, or you can make your own.

Herbs add symbolism and fragrance to the Advent wreath, one of the most beautiful pre-Christmas decorations. This wreath can be made in November, using herbs from your garden or from indoor pots.

Soak the sphagnum moss ring well and fill it with many short lengths of boxwood, each 4 inches long. Then add the herbs that are appropriate for this wreath because of their association with Biblical history; thyme, lavender, rosemary, hyssop, wormwood, lemon balm, mints, winter savory, southernwood, marjoram, and all sages are some of the herbs available in our garden in November. All the herbs, including the boxwood, must be conditioned by submerging them in a sinkful of warm, not hot, water before inserting them into the advent ring. Eventually, some of the cuttings will root in the damp sphagnum.

Place the wreath on a tray of pebbles for drainage and keep it damp. Store it, encased in plastic, outside every night until the hard frost arrives, and the wreath will enjoy a cold respite. Bring it indoors to enjoy during the day.

Add four candles, using candle holders inserted into the ring or set inside or along the perimeter of the wreath. The first candle (penitential purple for the color of the season) should be lighted with the evening meal on the first Saturday in Advent. Each week, light an additional candle (purple the second and fourth weeks, pink the third), until all four finally "light the way" for the prophecies of Christmas. Four white candles, symbols of joy and purity, may be used to replace the burned candles on Christmas Day.

Children delight in this old-world custom; their excitement mounts as the days pass.

# FIFTY HERBS

## Alpine Strawberry
### *(Fragaria semperflorens)**

Perennial, 1 foot

### How To Grow It

Fraises des Bois, the "Strawberry of the Woods," is a choice occupant for an herb garden. Be sure to include it in yours. Grown from seed, these strawberries traditionally make superb edging plants because they set no runners. Once started, and given agreeable conditions, these busy little plants will flower and fruit continuously from June to November. Moved indoors to a sunny windowsill, Alpine strawberry will produce twelve months of the year.

Clumps increase in size quite rapidly, so that established plants may be divided every spring to make enough plants to border a garden. Simply lift each clump, wash its root system, and carefully pull it apart into as many divisions as possible. Reset with the crown at ground level.

To develop the flavor of this delectable fruit, mulch with either straw or pine needles. Also, plant it near the herbs it likes best—lettuce, spinach, bush beans, pyrethrum, borage, and thyme.

---

* The commonly used English names of the herbs in the following pages are from the Merriam-Webster dictionary; the Latin names are from Hortus Third by the staff of the L. H. Bailey Hortorium of Cornell University (1976).

119

A conventional pottery strawberry jar is a perfect container for the Alpine strawberry, because it is a decorative conversation piece and will produce berries. An old barrel in which a dozen holes have been cut makes a dandy substitute for a strawberry jar and has a charm all its own. Place a length of perforated pipe or downspouting down the center (plug the bottom of the pipe), and fill the barrel with good, enriched soil, well packed around each plant. It's easiest to plant the berries while filling the barrel with soil; place one plant in each of the holes and several on top.

Water the plant thoroughly by filling the pipe. The holes will ensure an even distribution of water to each plant. To encourage a good harvest, you must also feed the plants regularly, preferably with a water-soluble fertilizer such as fish emulsion.

These plants will reward you with a remarkable crop of perfect, little, pointed, sweet, red berries rising high above the foliage.

## How to Use It

My favorite way to use Alpine strawberries is to pop them in my mouth as I am weeding around them and then to share some with the birds. Other uses are to garnish a fruit salad, make jam or sauce for ice cream, adorn a bowl of cold cereal, or any way you would use strawberries. Since they are small, it is not always possible to have large quantities at one time, so freeze them as you pick them if you want to accumulate enough for making jam. Otherwise, enjoy them daily while admiring their attractive form and sweet nature.

### Fraises Chantilly

| | |
|---|---|
| 1 1/2 | cups heavy cream |
| 2 to 4 | tablespoons powdered sugar |
| 1 | teaspoon pure vanilla extract |
| 1 | cup Alpine strawberries, washed, hulled, and halved |

120

Whip the cream until it begins to stiffen; add sugar and vanilla. Continue beating until stiff. Stir the strawberries into the bowl of whipped cream, smothering them. Pile the composition into pretty glasses, being careful to retain its pink and white character. Chill for 2 hours before serving. Makes 6 half-cup servings.

# Angelica
## (Angelica archangelica)

Biennial, 3-5 feet

## How To Grow It

Angelica, of the heavenly name, is a large, vigorous plant, which occupies semi-shaded, damp areas in the background of the herb garden. Indigenous to northern Europe, fields of this herb abound in Iceland, where it grows profusely. The plant has extremely large, hollow stems and heavily indented leaves. When it blooms it supports great masses of chartreuse umbels, which quickly turn into even more spectacular chartreuse, then brown, seedheads.

These seeds will self-sow where they prefer to grow, ours having chosen a place near the shade of the apple trees. If you harvest the seeds after they are thoroughly mature, they need extreme cold weather to germinate. Either sow them before the onset of winter or put them in the refrigerator for several weeks before planting. Growing angelica successfully from seed depends upon the freshness of the seeds and their exposure to cold temperatures. When kept cut back so that it is not allowed to flower or, especially, to set seed, angelica will sometimes remain in the garden for three years.

# How To Use It

"The Herb of the Angels" has been used in seemingly every way people could devise. Considered the most protective of herbs, angelica planted at each corner of the house assures the occupants of safety from pestilence, financial reverses, lightning, and the deviltry of witches. During the Renaissance, doctors administered angelica for the most severe maladies; its powers it was believed, were revealed by the angels and bordered on the supernatural.

As the herbalist Gerard puts it, all parts of angelica are edible "to them that are hungry." American colonists used the fragrant leaves for medicinal tea, in potpourris, and also as a flavoring. The hollow stems are candied, most often cut into thin slivers for decorating elegant cakes.

## Crystallized Angelica

| | |
|---|---|
| 24 | 6-inch pieces of angelica (the large hollow stalks, fresh) |
| 2 | cups water |
| 2 | cups granulated sugar |

To prepare the angelica, soak it in cold water for several hours; plunge it into boiling hot water until, when pressed with your fingers, all stringy parts are easily removed. Do this under cold water. Boil a simple syrup of the water and sugar. Place the prepared angelica in the hot syrup (225° F) for 24 hours; drain, reheat the syrup, and repeat three times. On the fourth day, boil the syrup and angelica at 245° F. Remove from heat; cool. Drain; sprinkle with sugar. Dry thoroughly (this may take two weeks); store in a tin. Keeps indefinitely.

# Anise
*(Pimpinella anisum)*

Annual, 1-2 feet

## How To Grow It

A rather delicate plant, anise has small pale green, deeply trident leaflets. It is best grown from seeds where you wish it to stay, enjoying some light shade. For best results, always plant anise and coriander seeds together; one strengthens the other, and both will thrive.

The pale yellow-to-white flowers are graceful, those of all the parsley family, producing the licorice-flavored seeds desired for seasoning.

## How To Use It

Gather the delicately anise-flavored leaves whenever available and use them fresh with fish, fruits, or in salads. The seeds, which are harvested later in the season, should be dried thoroughly and stored in dark jars with screw lids. Both seeds and leaves, dried, are worthy additions to potpourri.

Add a few leaves to the water in which you steam shellfish; the seeds may be added to bread and Christmas cookie dough.

The seeds are also grown commercially to produce Anisette, a liqueur that you can duplicate by experimentally combining anise seeds and pure-grain alcohol or brandy. Bruise the seeds, add an ounce of seeds to a pint of liquid, and let it stand several months to a year.

123

## Simple Knot Design

1. Roman wood
2. Sweet Violet
3. Lavender
4. Germander

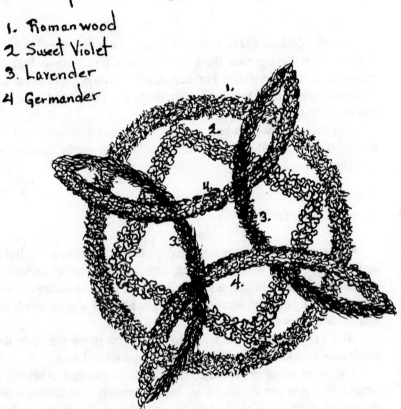

### *Anise Sugar*

| 1 | tablespoon anise seed |
|---|---|
| 1 | cup sugar |

Place ingredients in a blender and blend at high speed for a few minutes. Store in a moisture-proof jar for use in tea, on cookies, or with fruit. (This can, of course, be made the old way in a mortar with pestle.)

**Basil** *(Ocimum basilicum)* — Annual, 1-3 feet
**Dwarf Basil** *(Ocimum basilicum 'Minimum')* — Annual, 1 foot
**Purple Basil** *(Ocimum basilicum var. 'Dark Opal')* — Annual, 1 1/2-2 feet

Sweet Basil

**How To Grow It**

Sweet basil is one of the most popular culinary herbs—fragrant, handsome in the garden, and tasty. An annual of almost shrubby growth, basil can be clipped many times during the one-season growing year. Like tomatoes, it requires a hot, sunny position in the garden. In fact, you should grow basil and tomatoes together to keep the tomatoes free of many pesky invaders.

Easily grown from seed, basil sprouts in less than a week and then is off to a running start. It grows speedily, enjoying pot culture on a sunny window.

If you start basil indoors, don't be in a hurry to put it out in the garden. Wait until all danger of frost is over and it's time to plant tomatoes, which require warm soil. In the meantime, basil will thrive on your sunniest windowsill where you can use it in your salads. When it gets too big, break off four-inch pieces, which quickly root in damp vermiculite and give you bonus plants.

The dwarf basil is very attractive as an edging in the herb garden, growing, as it does, in small mounds of pale green foliage, a form that also lends itself to pot culture. A dark red variety called "Dark Opal" makes a striking color contrast in the herb garden, particularly when planted with gray santolinas or rue "Blue Beauty." Planting these two together is against Culpeper's advice when he writes, "this herb and rue will not grow together." Test this interesting theory yourself.

New varieties appear annually—holly, licorice, cinnamon, camphor, lemon, Picollo and picture perfect Spicy Globe, to name a few. We like to plant a basil garden on our door stoop, using as many kinds as we can acquire in assorted large containers.


## How To Use It

Gather and use fresh basil daily from the garden all summer, drying the surplus for winter use. In fact, basil must be kept cut or it will go to seed, terminating its life cycle soon after.

Snippets of the tasty anise-flavored leaves are mandatory in tomato recipes, but try it also in soups, stews, meat loaf, zucchini, eggplant, fish, and all Italian dishes and sauces. Try a pinch of basil in a pound cake.

Basil makes an excellent vinegar. Just harvest the tops in August, pour over them heated white vinegar, and steep the vinegar for two weeks. We grow the red basil especially for this purpose; it creates a tasty vinegar, colored sparkling burgundy-pink. Yes, the "Dark Opal" basil is edible even though it is most frequently listed as ornamental in seed catalogs.

The smell of basil is "good for the heart and the head," so use it in bath waters and potpourri and as a tea to quiet the nerves. A sprig of basil tucked behind your ear while you work in the garden will keep gnats and other pesky insects away while perfuming your task. Pots of basil may be grown around patios and picnic areas to repel mosquitoes and flies. This works extremely well. We occasionally demonstrate candy-making—what could be more enticing to flies? A few portable pots of basil take care of the problem very nicely indeed.

The house surrounded by basil is blessed, so waft your hands over it every chance you get. The aromatic herb will envelop you in good smells. Since basil enjoys stroking, no wonder ours grows so well; I can't keep my hands off it!

### Basil Spaghetti Sauce (or Pesto)

| | |
|---|---|
| 2 | generous handfuls of green basil leaves |
| 1 | cup pine nuts (walnuts or almonds may be substituted) |
| 4 | cloves garlic |
| 4 | ounces Parmesan cheese, grated |
| 1 | cup olive oil |

Place all ingredients in a blender; blend 1 minute on high speed. Serve at room temperature over very hot pasta. Serves 6.

# Bay Laurel
## *(Laurus nobilis)*

Tender Perennial, 6 feet

## How To Grow It

The true laurel of history and the poets (commonly called bay tree, or simply bay, sometimes sweet bay), bay laurel has glossy evergreen leaves, which are both beautiful and useful. Bay is usually grown in tubs to make it easier to move outside in summer and inside in winter, or, in milder climates, to wherever it is most decorative in the garden.

An evergreen that responds well to clipping, bay can be grown as a pyramidal tree or as a standard. In the Mediterranean region, where it is native, bay is a tree that reaches forty feet. From Virginia south, bay can be grown outdoors to lend dignity to the landscape, a splendid feature for the herb garden.

Bay is, however, very slow growing. It tolerates houseplant conditions to a degree impossible with most other herbs, especially if it isn't confined to a hot room and is given plenty of moisture during its summer growing season. Bay will, in fact, withstand considerable neglect and adverse conditions as long as it is kept in a cool room.

If the bay you grow is troubled with an occasional bout of scaly insects, scrape off the pests and wipe the underside of the leaves with a cotton pad doused in alcohol, an effective control. Washing the glossy leaves with a strong yellow soap is always good insurance.

Clipping maintains the shapeliness of bay. The clippings become your harvest or cuttings to root. Ah, the rooting of bay! We do it with as much success as failure. Rooting is interminably slow. Take cuttings after the new growth hardens, in July. Using a sharp knife, gently scrape the bottom inch of the wood, dip the wood into rooting hormone (one designed for hardwood cuttings), and firm it into place

128

in the best possible soil you can provide—under the shade of a low-growing tree or shrub where it will receive light but no sun. Keep it moist, not wet.

Rooting is slow and uncertain; but, in the case of bay, success is sweet and well worth waiting for. By September the cuttings should be ready to be transferred into a flat of good soil where root growth will continue indoors in a cool room during the winter months—again, if it is not kept too wet. New leaves in the spring indicate success; another bay plant is ready to grow. Pot it up and glow with pride.

Individual leaves may be harvested and dried in a warm, dark place for use in cooking or to make a victory crown (see index), as you prefer. Store the dry leaves in a tightly-lidded container where they will keep indefinitely.


## How To Use It

The noble bay, symbol of victory and triumph, honor and glory, was once believed to be powerfully imbued with mystical properties, as protection against witches, evil spirits, thunder, and lightning. Traditionally, crowns of laurel were accorded poets, scholars, and triumphant athletes.

Today's cook will win praise by using the bay laurel leaf in stew. The flavor of the mighty bay can be dominating, so use it with caution. One bay leaf is usually adequate for stew, casserole, soup, or spaghetti for six. Remove the leaf when cooking is completed.

Medieval cooks used bay, juniper berries, horseradish, and other measures to flavor wild game meats or those which had been around too long. Suckling pig, boiled boar, roast hare, fish stews, beef, lamb, and pork are only a few of the main dishes that benefit by the addition of bay.

For centuries the bay has been used as a weevil repellent. From biblical times the housewife struggled to keep bothersome insects out of her starchy staples; she treasured the leaves of bay for this purpose. Put several whole bay leaves in your canisters of rice, noodles, cereals, and flour as well as with such spices as cinnamon, paprika, and nutmeg. Don't expect one bay leaf to do the work of many in a very large container; use several, keeping them whole so that they can be reused in another canister or used in cookery. Bay is a powerful protective, witches or weevils.

The French have an easy way to add and subtract the bay leaf—the *bouquet garni* , a bunch of herbs tied together and lowered into the soup on a long string. Dried herbs may be put into squares of cheesecloth and used in the same manner. A clever Christmas gift, fun to make and give, a collection of *bouquets garnis* could be presented in a prettily decorated jar.

## Bouquet Garni

| 12 | whole bay leaves |
| 12 | teaspoons whole celery seeds |
| 24 | whole cloves |
| 36 | peppercorns |
| 12 | tablespoons dried parsley |
| 6 | teaspoons thyme |

Divide the above ingredients equally onto 12, 4-inch square pieces of muslin or new cheesecloth. Tie with heavy white twine, leaving a long string attached for easy removal at the end of the cooking time.

## Margaret's Pastrami

4 to 6     pound brisket of corned beef

130

| 4 | onions, each stuck with 6 whole cloves |
|---|---|
| 1/8 | cup peppercorns |
| 4 | carrots |
| 1 | bay leaf |
| 1 | teaspoon ground allspice |
| 1/2 | teaspoon ground cloves |
| 1 | teaspoon ground pepper |
| 1/2 | cup brown sugar |

Barely cover the brisket with water. Add the onions, peppercorns, carrots, and bay leaf. Simmer for an hour or so. Meanwhile, combine spices and sugar. Transfer the beef to a roasting pan and rub it with the spice and sugar mixture. Bake at 325º F for 3 to 4 hours or until tender, basting frequently with the court bouillon in which it was first simmered. Serve hot or cold.

**Note:** It is important to know that the words *bay* and/or *laurel* are used in reference to many different plants and do not always refer to the true bay, *Laurus nobilis*. Mountain laurel, the state flower of Pennsylvania, is *Kalmia latifolia*, lovely to look at in the mountains; but the leaves, which look like bay, are poisonous. Bay rum is made from oil of bay, distilled from a West Indian plant, *Pimenta acris*. Bayberries are harvested from *Myrica pensylvanica* or *Myrica cerifera*, a glossy evergreen shrub that abounds along our Atlantic coastal area, bearing gray berries from which we get the wax for bayberry candles. The leaves are highly aromatic but bitter and are not used in cooking. Cherry laurel (*Prunus caroliniana*), an elegant native, has useful, glossy evergreen leaves and can easily be mistaken for bay laurel, but, again, it can be poisonous. California bay laurel is *Umbellularia californica*. It is very similar to the true bay, extremely handsome, grown in tubs as an ornamental along the streets of San Francisco and a good substitute for the true *Laurus nobilis*. It is usually labeled California bay laurel.

131

# Borage
## (*Borago officinalis*)

Hardy Annual, 3 feet

## How To Grow It

There are few problems with growing borage; simply sow the seeds and borage will grow, providing you have given it a sunny place. After you have started it in your garden, borage will pop up wherever it prefers to be. We welcome borage anywhere it wants to grow, which is never in the same place twice; it skips about in the garden, surprising us with the places it selects and giving us those heavenly blue star flowers to ponder upon. These flowers are borne by a central stock that emerges from large, rough leaves. Related to comfrey, forget-me-not, and bugloss, borage has a large family of useful blue-eyed cousins.

Keep borage cut back, and it will continue to bloom throughout the summer. Otherwise, it will self-sow a second crop, the first very early in the year and a second later in the fall with larger, bluer flowers on sturdier stalks. Obviously, it likes cool evenings and sunny days.

Borage is a bee herb. It does not like to be transplanted and is not in favor of life in a pot.

## How To Use It

At one time borage was grown medicinally as an antidepressant, for fevers, and to "bring always courage." We find it cheering just to see borage in bloom in the garden.

It takes courage to eat the large, rough, mildly cucumber-flavored leaves, but we have added the very young, tender ones to our green salads, fish salads, and fruit salads, where they make an attractive garnish. However, speaking of garnishes, don't waste one

132

of the lovely flowers, they are the brightest blue imaginable, a startling contrast to food on a platter. Besides this, they add flavor to drinks. Dickens, it is said, considered no claret cup worth drinking without borage.

### Candied Borage Blossoms

Gather the largest, freshest borage blossoms available, wash them, and lay them on an absorbent towel to drain. Whip one egg white until frothy. Using a soft brush, apply the egg white to both sides of each blossom. Lay the blossoms on waxed paper and sift finely granulated sugar over them. Allow them to set for a few minutes, turn them over, and cover their undersides with sugar. Air-dry them for ten days to two weeks before packing them away in airtight, moisture-proof tins. Serve on trays with Christmas cookies.

## Burnet, Salad
### (Poterium sanguisorba)

Perennial, 1 foot

The dense clumps of burnet compound leaflets hug the ground, producing hundreds of flavorful leaves to use and enjoy. In spring, burnet erupts into flower—tall stems of nondescript, reddish ovals

133

that become burred seeds willing to self-sow everywhere. Cut back the flowers if you do not want an army of volunteer burnets.

I have never succeeded in dividing burnet to propagate it vegetatively, so I recommend that it be grown from seed, which is easily done in early spring, indoors or out. Plant it in full sun in the foreground of the herb garden.

## How To Use It

We wouldn't want to be without burnet in the garden or in the kitchen. The"dyspeptic's cucumber," burnet smiles on those who cannot normally take cucumbers in their diet. Burnet smells and tastes like cucumbers, and can be used in dips or salads in place of them with no after effects—perhaps the reason it "doth comfort and rejoice the hart."

No need to dry burnet; it loses its flavor when dried, anyway. Instead, gather fresh leaves any time you want to toss them in a salad. The harvest continues all year; even under heavy snows, where the leaves remain as crisp and succulent as if they were in your refrigerator. You may also use burnet in sandwiches and dips, mixed with creamed or cottage cheese, as garnishes, and in herb vinegars or butters.

### Burnet Finger Sandwiches

| | |
|---|---|
| 8 | ounces cream cheese |
| 2 | tablespoons mayonnaise |
| 1/3 | cup chives, finely snipped |
| 1/2 | cup burnet leaves, snipped |

134

Soften the cream cheese with the mayonnaise and add the herbs. Mix thoroughly. Spread on 12 slices of thinly-sliced bread, crusts removed; cover with 12 more slices of bread and cut in fancy shapes.

### Burnet Dip

| | |
|---|---|
| 1 | pint sour cream |
| 1 | cup chopped burnet leaves |
| 1 | shallot, finely minced |

Mix all ingredients together. Marinate for several hours, salt if necessary, and serve with crispy crackers. Garnish the dip with several attractive burnet leaves. At Christmas, touch up the dip with bits of red pimiento.

### Burnet Vinegar

| | |
|---|---|
| 1 | pint burnet leaves |
| 1/4 | cup lovage (leaves only) |
| 1 | cup parsley |
| 1/4 | cup onion tops |
| 1 | quart apple cider vinegar |

Place all the herbs, whole, in a large glass jar (a gallon pickle jar works well). Heat the vinegar, but not to a boil, and pour it over the herbs. Stand in sun for two weeks. Strain and put into smaller bottles. Add a sprig of the herb burnet for attractiveness. Label.

# Calendula, Pot Marigold
*(Calendula officinalis)*

Annual, 1 foot

## How To Grow It

You will recognize calendula, or pot marigold, as the little, single-petaled orange daisy that sows itself all over grandmother's flower garden. It is a useful little annual, which makes itself at home wherever you plant it and some places that you haven't.

Calendula requires no special care except full sun. Its name means "herb of the sun" because it is known to have bloomed during every month, its bright flowers opening only on sunny days. The "winking Marybuds" of Shakespeare's day, calendula was called the "marigold that goes to bed wi' th' sun." Sun-loving calendula closes its flower heads when they are picked for bouquets, at night, or on cloudy days in the garden.

Calendula will flower longer if all its dead flowers are removed, which is your harvest. When the seeds ripen on the remaining flowers, gather them for the following year or simply allow them to self-sow, in which case you will need to thin them to ten or twelve inches apart in the spring when they again appear in the garden. Plant Calendula in the culinary, the medicinal, the dye, or the tea garden.

## How to Use it

A multitude of recipes, both culinary and cosmetic, calling for marigolds have appeared in various publications. They refer to pot marigold, the herb calendula, not to the strong-smelling French and African marigolds (which are neither French nor African, but native to the Americas) now developed into many fancy hybrids and planted

136

in summer gardens for their glorious color. I'm sure these would taste as strong as they smell.

Calendula is called pot marigold because it is suitable for use in the cooking pot, where it may be used generously. Calendula is a golden addition to broths, split pea soup, tossed green salads, scrambled eggs, and custard. It imparts its color to breads, dumplings, and cakes, and it sometimes used as a substitute for the more costly saffron.

Calendula tea was once used as a simply remedy for reducing fever and bringing out the measles in children. It is still a European favorite for children's ailments, not only as a tea, but in diaper rash creams, baby powders, and soothing lotions. When you are working in the garden, you may use calendula blossoms for first aid for the sting of any insect.

When boiled, the flowers yield a yellow dye; when dried, they add color and bulk to potpourri. Gather all you can grow.

### Soothing Ointment

| | |
|---|---|
| 1/2 | cup cold cream |
| 1/2 | cup pot marigold petals, fresh or dried |

Melt the cold cream over very low heat; add the petals. Keep in a jar for use as a healing facial cream or for first aid.

### Calendula Butter

| | |
|---|---|
| 1/2 | cup calendula blossoms |
| 1 | cup (2 sticks) butter, softened |

| 3 | tablespoons sour cream |
|---|---|
| 3 | tablespoons orange marmalade |

Separate petals from the flower centers; carefully wash and drain the petals before combining them with the butter, sour cream and marmalade. Mix thoroughly. Spread on slices of bread, with crusts removed. Cut into finger sandwiches. This butter is especially good on Swedish Limpa bread.

| | |
|---|---|
| **Chamomile, Roman** | Sometimes |
| *(Chamaemelum nobilis)* | perennial, 1 foot |
| **Chamomile, German** | Annual, 1 foot |
| *(Matricaria recutita)* | |

## How To Grow It

"The more it is trodden on, the faster it grows," Shakespeare says about chamomile. This is true only if the climate suites this low-growing, daisy-flowered herb. It will not thrive where it is dry, windswept, or extremely cold. Where conditions are right, however, you will have a unique lawn with less mowing, plus a crop of fragrant, useful flowers.

If the climate does not promote growth, settle for a patch of chamomile in the herb garden, gathering the little flower heads as they appear. Chamomile is easily grown from seed but seems to resent both pot culture and transplanting. An open, sunny location with good drainage is best.

Prepare the seedbed by cultivating the soil to a depth of several inches. Spread the infinitesimal seeds about, barely scratching them in. Cover the area with a damp cloth until germination takes place in about ten days.

The ferny leaves will be quickly followed by small, white daisies. The golden centers of the daisies are the harvest. Gather and dry the flowers several times each summer. In the process, the white petals will drop off, but it doesn't really matter.

When chamomile escapes the garden and grows naturally, let it flourish in its chosen home. The wild chamomile is preferred, so count yourself lucky.

## How to Use It

Chamomile tea is what Mrs. Rabbit gave to Peter, that naughty bunny, when he came out of Mr. McGregor's cabbage patch. She wished to ward off a possible cold. The tea is made by steeping 2 teaspoons of the herb to a cup of boiling water for five to ten minutes, depending upon the strength desired. Both tonic and sedative, chamomile is especially good for nerves or as a nightcap. It is a tea with calming influences. Honey and milk can be added to the hot, amber brew. Chamomile tea can be enjoyed alone or combined with other herbs such as mint, fennel, linden blossoms, or catnip.

Steeped in boiling water until cool, chamomile is also nature's own cosmetic counter. Strain the strong infusion and use it as a skin toner by alternating hot and cold compresses of the tea. It is astringent enough to effect a smooth complexion, radiant and youthful, famous in European beauty spas.

If your hair has a blonde tint, a chamomile rinse will bring out the golden highlights, especially when you hair is dried outdoors in full sun. Chamomile is a natural dye, so prolonged use will do no harm but will keep blonde hair colored naturally.

The same tea or infusion when rubbed on exposed parts of the body will repel insects—a good tip when you are working in the garden. Carry along a bottle of chamomile lotion when you vacation at the shore.

## *Chamomile Shampoo*

1    cup chamomile blossoms
1    pint water, boiled
1    pint castile shampoo

Steep the chamomile blossoms in boiled water until cool. Strain through cloth and add to the shampoo. Use on light hair as often as you like.

## Catnip
*(Nepeta cataria)*
## Nepeta
*(Nepeta mussini)*

Perennial, 1 to 3 ft.

Perennial, 1 foot

*Catnip*

### How to Grow It

The colonists brought catnip to America because they relished it as a substitute for scarce Oriental teas. Now we recognize the same catnip as one of our most common and persistent weeds of the fields. A pungent mint that kitty adores, catnip thrives on utmost neglect, self-sows everywhere, and is hardly suitable for the patterned herb garden.

A more refined form is nepeta, or nept, a hardy, low-growing perennial with soft, lavender blooms from earliest spring to late frost. Keep nepeta cut back to maintain its lovely, circular form and continuous flowering.

Grow catnip, the common variety, in a pot on a sunny windowsill as a treat for a pet cat. Keep new plants coming along at all times, as cats enjoy this healthy treat daily. Both catnip and fancier nepeta are easily grown from seed or root divisions of established plants.

# How to Use It

Catnip is often grown near chicken houses and other farm buildings where mice are a problem on the theory that it will attract cats who will eliminate the rodents. In return for this service, you may gather the wild or tame sorts of catnip, combine and dry them well, crumble the leaves together, and stuff soft balls or fish or mice made from scraps of felt for your cat. Kitty won't be at all fussy about your handiwork as she romps with this toy.

Catnip tea has been used medicinally for centuries. As an aid to digestion, it can be enjoyed before, during and after a meal. It is also a mild stimulant, and a tonic considered useful in building resistance to colds. Fretful babies love it's calming influence.

## *Catnip Tea*

Steep 1 tsp. dried catnip per cup of boiling water, plus 1 teaspoon for the pot, for 3 to 5 minutes. Serve with sugar or honey and lemon, iced in summer, hot in winter. This mintlike tea is especially good for anyone who cannot take the stimulus of regular teas.

# Chervil
*(Anthriscus cerefolium)*

Annual 1 foot

## How to Grow It

Delicately flavored, delicately leaved, chervil is an elegant plant but a shy one. Plant them in partial shade, and do not disturb them once they have germinated. The seeds may be sown as they ripen or early in the spring. Occasionally they will self-sow. Chervil may also be grown in a pot on the windowsill, where it makes a dainty plant with an anise flavor. It is grown only from seed.

A short-lived annual with lacy, double-compound leaves and small, whitish flowers, when grown in strong sun, chervil will burn a reddish brown, quickly go to seed, and perish.

## How to Use It

Chervil can be used in nearly everything, especially those recipes in which you normally use parsley. Sometimes referred to as "French parsley," chervil leaves are chopped into salads, soups, and sauces (especially bearnaise sauce), and added to cucumbers.

Since good dried chervil is difficult to find, I advise gathering your own tender leaves, then air-drying them out of the sun on clean, white paper to store for later use.

Once used in the treatment of gout and as an aid to digestion, this attractive plant is now considered the gourmet's herb, almost totally confined to use in the kitchen. It is always included in that mixture of finely minced herbs referred to as *fines herbes*.

## *Les Fines Herbes*

| | |
|---|---|
| 1 | cup parsley |
| 1 | cup chervil |
| 1/2 | cup tarragon |
| 1/2 | cup chives |

Chop fresh herbs finely; dry thoroughly; store in a tightly lidded, dark container. Use in sauces, salads, chicken, broths, or butter.

## *Les Fines Herbes Butter*

| | |
|---|---|
| 2 | tablespoons *fines herbes* (above) |
| 1 | tablespoon minced fresh chives |
| 1/4 | pound butter (or butter substitute) |

Mix herbs and butter thoroughly and allow to mellow together for 24 hours. Serve on hot biscuits, vegetables, or matzos.

# Chive
*(Allium schoenoprasum)*

Perennial, 1 1/2 foot

Chives

## How to Grow It

Favorite edging plants in the herb garden, chives are mild onions, as indispensable to cookery as to their neighbors in the garden. Since chives are rarely attacked by diseases or insects, vegetable plants near them are also blessed with great vigor and health. As with most alliums, the roots exude a substance repellent to insects.

Plant chives from seed or divide an established clump to make a whole row of chives, which are showy when they bloom. Remember to plant them in small groups; chives prefer being plural. The mature clumps need to be divided every three years, or they will crowd themselves out. Good drainage and full sun are the requisites. Chives also appreciate being cut back drastically several times during the growing year lest they become too tall and flop over. Otherwise, they are easy to grow, very hardy, and no trouble.

To grow them on the windowsill in winter, pot chives taken from the garden and winterize them on an outside porch or in a cold frame until February or March, when they can be brought inside to begin life anew. This cold rest period is absolutely essential to success. Potted chives should not, of course, dry out.

Chives, once forced, can be harvested for several months, then should be returned to the garden to renew their exhausted bulbs.

Drying the lovely, green chive harvest can be disappointing; chives usually fade to straw color and lose their flavor. When you crop a clump of chives, the fistful of tubular green tops can be stored in a plastic bag in the refrigerator for over a week while you use and enjoy them on nearly everything you cook. If you have an abundant harvest, freeze the surplus for winter use by snipping the washed herb onto a cookie sheet, freezing quickly, and storing in a freezer container to use as needed.

## How to Use It

Cut the thin, long chive leaves by the inch and snip into smaller pieces. Use chopped chives on baked potatoes, in sour cream, in dips, as an addition to butter, to garnish cottage cheese or potato salad, and wherever a delicate onion flavor is desired.

One of the best sellers at a recent herb sale was a delicate lavender colored vinegar in a pretty bottle. It was made in May with chive blossoms.

### *Pink Chive Blossom Vinegar*

Fill a quart jar with fresh chive blossoms; pour over hot, not boiling, white vinegar and steep in full sun for two weeks. Strain and bottle. The vinegar may be diluted if you find chive blossoms too strong for your taste. This pungent vinegar is for sauces, salads, red beets, and food sales. Bottle it prettily, apply a label, and it will sell exceedingly well.

# Comfrey
## (*Symphytum officinale*)

Perennial, 5 foot or
more

## How to Grow It

Comfrey has a long, honorable history of service to people and should be included in every herb garden. If it is too large for your garden, put it in the shrubbery border or back by the compost pile, where it will act as a screen.

No special instructions are necessary to grow comfrey successfully. It prefers full sun and grows well in any soil, its deep roots penetrating many feet. Insects and plant diseases are absolutely no problem when it is in the small garden.

Comfrey can be started from seeds or preferably from root divisions; almost every two-inch piece of the root will sprout, and grow into a large plant. This herb needs plenty of room so the roots should be planted about three feet apart. After the second year you will be able to harvest each comfrey plant, and by the third year three to five harvests during the growing season are not unusual, each yielding about a bushel of nitrogen-rich leaves per plant. Keep comfrey back to within four inches of the soil. This will seem ruthless, but it must be done. The plant immediately puts forth new, vigorous growth, which in turn becomes your next harvest. If comfrey is not cut back, it will flop over and send up new growth from the central crown. It will also go to seed, and soon will be growing everywhere.

Comfrey is also a remarkable houseplant. If grown in a sunny window, it will not achieve its customary gigantic proportions but will remain a nice-sized plant, producing tender, fresh green leaves for salads or for first aid. Pot plants of comfrey need to be fertilized.

147

# How to Use It

Comfrey is the gardener's best friend. The large leaves make a highly nitrogenous green manure, which can be dug right into the soil, used as a mulch, or added to the compost pile, where it becomes an activating agent, quickly turning the other vegetable debris into a rich fluffy soil conditioner.

The young, tender leaves, which come up very early in spring, are delicious cooked like spinach or chopped into green salads, especially those prepared with a hot bacon dressing.

Comfrey is an ancient medicinal herb used officially for burns, wounds, lung diseases, ulcers, and broken bones. Its botanical name, *symphytum,* means "to grow together" and refers to this last employment. "Knitbone," its common name, means the same thing.

Comfrey leaves are an invaluable addition to animal fodder; all animals benefit by this enrichment of their diet. Caged songbirds respond to a biweekly comfrey leaf treat by bursting into song, so be sure to grow it indoors in winter if you have a canary.

## Comfrey Juice Cocktail

| | |
|---|---|
| 6 | large comfrey leaves |
| 1 | large can unsweetened pineapple juice |

Thoroughly blend ingredients in a blender, set at highest speed. Strain and serve chilled. You may add other herbs such as parsley, celery tops, and leftover juices, to vary this bright green, healthful drink. It's pretty for breakfast!

## Comfrey Tea

Harvest young tender green leaves and dry them in the oven slowly. Pack them away in tightly lidded containers to use as tea.

1 teaspoon. crumbled comfrey leaves
1 cup boiling water

Pour the water over the leaves, steep 10 minutes, and sweeten if desired.

### Irish Potato Salad

6 cup boiled diced potatoes
4 eggs, boiled 4 minutes and cut in small pieces
1 teaspoon. sea kelp
1/2 cup vegetable oil
1 teaspoon honey
1/2 cup plums
1 1/2 cups chopped green comfrey

Put the potatoes in a bowl with the eggs, the sea kelp, and the oil. Mix well. Add the honey to the plums and stir well with the chopped comfrey. Thoroughly combine the potato mixture with the comfrey and plums.

# Coriander
*(Coriandrum sativum)*

Annual, 1-3 feet

## How to Grow It

Coriander is another herb used by many cultures. Mentioned in the Bible, this ancient herb is a zesty addition to all cuisines. Its folk name, "Chinese parsley," is indicative of its universal appeal.

Grown for its leaves as well as for its round, yellowish-brown fruits, this popular *umbellifer* prefers hot weather and dry soil. In May, sow the seeds where it is to grow, as it does not like to be transplanted. Thin coriander so the plants are one inch apart. We sow anise and coriander seeds together for mutual strength and support.

After harvesting the leaves, dry them for later use. Gather the seeds when ripe—about the end of August. Store leaves and seeds separately in dark, airtight containers. They are two uniquely different seasonings.

## How to Grow It

If you enjoy South American, Mexican, or Indian cookery, your best source of the strong seasoning known as *cilantro* is a pot of coriander seedlings growing on your sunny windowsill. Cut the leaves as needed. Be sure to keep a supply of the seedlings coming along.

The seeds are used in pickling spices, as an addition to Scandinavian gingerbread, making it even spicier, in curry powder, and candied for an old-fashioned treat. Children suck on the sugary little balls called "comfits," until they bite into the peppery coriander seed in the center—an exciting contrast in flavors!

150

## *Herb Cookies*

| | |
|------|-----------------------------|
| 1/2 | cup butter or margarine |
| 1/2 | cup sugar |
| 1 | egg |
| 1/2 | cup molasses |
| 2 1/4 | cups sifted flour |
| 2 | teaspoons baking soda |
| 3 | teaspoons ginger |
| 1 | teaspoon cinnamon |
| 1/2 | teaspoon cloves |
| 1/4 | teaspoon salt |
| 1/3 | cup strongly brewed coffee |
| 2 | tablespoons anise seed |
| 2 | teaspoons ground coriander seed |

In a mixing bowl, cream butter and sugar until light and fluffy; add egg and blend well. Beat in the molasses. In a separate bowl, combine flour, soda, ginger, cinnamon, cloves, and salt, and add alternately with the black coffee to the butter mixture. Add anise seed and coriander, blending well. Drop by rounded measuring teaspoonsful two inches apart onto lightly greased baking sheets. Bake at 350° F for 8-10 minutes or until firm. Remove to racks and let cool thoroughly before storing in airtight tins. Makes 6 dozen.

# Costmary
## (*Chrysanthemum balsamita*)

Perennial, 2-3 feet

## How to Grow It

"Sweet Mary" smells and tastes like a popular brand of chewing gum. It has a delicious, mintlike flavor. A fragrant perennial with long, straplike leaves, pale green and lovely, costmary likes full sun and good drainage. Do not allow it to be shaded by adjacent plants. Every third year, divide roots in the spring by digging up the plant and allowing it to fall into several pieces, which can then be reset. The flowers are buttonlike, unexciting, and rarely set seed.

The names costmary and Sweet Mary refer to the plant's association with the Virgin Mary, probably because it is one of the herbs that blooms during church festivals in her honor.

We have changed costmary's location in our garden several times over the course of the years to find a spot it will accept. We have also learned to winter over, in the cold frame, at least one plant of costmary to be sure of a supply in the spring. Don't feel badly if costmary doesn't grow for you. This herb seems to have a choosy disposition.

## How to Use It

In colonial days, costmary was called "Bible leaf" because the long leaves made ideal bookmarks in hymnals, marking the passage and exuding a delightful fragrance during endless hours of prayer and sermonizing. It is also an excellent deterrent for such book bugs as silver fish. Keep a leaf in every volume in your library.

The leaves have been used medicinally in the past to make a not unpleasant tea for the stomach. We gather and dry a great deal of the leaves for potpourri, in which they retain their fragrance for a long

152

time. Because they are insect repellant, dried costmary leaves and lavender stems tied together are kept with stored linens.

We have one rare recipe using costmary in meatballs—a tantalizing addition to ordinary fare. Try a pinch in your own favorite hamburger recipe. Costmary has also been used sparingly in salads, and in various drinks to which it contributes a lot. Sometimes called "alecost," costmary was traditionally used to flavor ale.

### Old Ale Posset

| | |
|---|---|
| 1 | quart ale |
| 2 | tablespoons sugar |
| 1/2 | teaspoon ground ginger |
| 2 | costmary leaves |
| 1 | quart milk |

Heat the ale, sugar, ginger and leaves. Heat the milk separately. Remove the leaves and mix both liquids together. Stir until frothy and serve with grated nutmeg.

# Dill
*(Anethum graveolens)*

Annual, 3-4 feet

## How to Grow it

One of the herbs best grown from seeds, dill is planted in spring as early as March or in summer, if one wishes a later crop. It should be sown where you want it to grow. Easy to grow, dill strongly resents being disturbed; it will reward your transplanting efforts with lackadaisical growth.

Seeds from your pantry shelf can be used to grow a fresh dill crop if they are less than three years old. To sow, simply drill a shallow row in the vegetable garden or sprinkle the seeds sparsely in a well-prepared, sunny bed. The feathery annual will germinate in a week or so, producing tall, hollow stalks bearing savory leaves called "dill weed." You will have a good crop of new, tasty seeds in about two months. Collect all but a few of the seedheads for use during pickle season, dry the rest for later, and allow some of the seeds to self-sow.

If dill is happy where you grow it in your garden, it will re-seed itself in the same general area, coming up far lustier than the first stand, no matter how carefully it was planted initially. Take advantage of this unique, built-in ability of dill to adapt to your particular garden and always allow some of your dill to self-sow. After five or six years it may need to be replenished with fresh seeds sown in a different part of the garden.

## How to Use It

Protection against witchcraft, a soothing tea for colicky babies, flavor for favorite pickles—what more could one ask? Dill is all of

154

this and more, so grow lots of dill in your herb garden.

All the ancient herbalists agreed on the value of dill in the treatment of hiccoughs, but each had a different method of application. The seeds could be tied in a cloth, boiled in wine, and smelled; another herbalist advocated drinking a tea of the seeds and leaves; and yet another recommended simply nibbling the seeds.

The name dill comes from an old Anglo-Saxon word "dilla," which means "to dull," because of its ability to soothe pain. A mild sedative, "dill water" was described in a seventeenth-century herbal as soothing to infants. The colonist's wife also made hard little dill-seed cakes for her teething babies.

Fresh young leaves are to be savored, so much so that snippets from dill seeds sprouting on a sunny windowsill during the winter will add pleasant flavor to cottage cheese, cream cheese, new potatoes, and scrambled eggs. Plant a dozen or more seeds to a six-inch pot, and place in a sunny windowsill to have some dill weed for cooking. Do not expect seeds from these little plants; replace them by planting additional seeds as often as necessary.

All egg dishes can be made tantalizing by dill weed or dill seed, deviled eggs in particular. Pot roast, lamb stew, roast pork, shellfish, creamed chicken, and hamburger all benefit from a pinch of aromatic dill. Tomato, split pea, and most other kings of soup, especially borscht, need dill. Any recipe that has become a bit tiresome can be sparked by this remarkable ancient herb.

Dill has so many culinary uses, it's hard to know where to begin or end. Two excellent recipes that can give the sweetly pungent flavor of dill to almost any dish are dill vinegar and dill butter.

Dill vinegar is made by pouring hot, not boiling, vinegar over dill seeds, fresh from the garden or off the grocer's shelf, and allowing it to steep for two weeks. Strain and bottle the vinegar to flavor salads, sauces, gravies, red beets, or green beans. The vinegar preserves the essential oil of the dill and is the next best thing to using the fresh herb. Today's busy housewife can save the juice from store-bought pickles and do the same thing.

Dill butter is another easy favorite. It is made with finely minced dill weed (the thinnings from the garden are perfect for this, as they have a more delicate flavor than the seeds). Mix three tablespoons into a quarter of a pound of butter, blend, and mellow for several days. Try this on hot toast or muffins for lunch, and you'll be delighted by the piquant flavor. Add it to boiled, cubed new potatoes for a quick version of Swedish dilled potatoes.

Other vegetables improved by the light touch of dill, especially in dill butter, include cabbage, carrots, zucchini, tomatoes, turnips, eggplant, squash, and lima beans.

## Blender Dill Sauce

| | |
|---|---|
| 1 | cup diced unpeeled cucumber |
| 2 | tablespoons lemon juice |
| 1 | teaspoon onion salt |
| 1/4 | teaspoon celery salt |
| 1/2 | teaspoon dill seed (or 1 T. dill weed) |

Combine all ingredients in the blender for about 30 seconds, or cover and blend until the cucumber is smoothly blended. Pour this mixture gradually into a combination of:

| | |
|---|---|
| 1/3 | cup sour cream |
| 1/3 | cup mayonnaise |

Stir constantly until blended. Makes 1 1/3 cups sauce. Dill sauce is excellent with fish, especially salmon.

## Dillicious Pickles

| | |
|---|---|
| 3 | cup white vinegar |
| 3 | cup water |
| 1/3 | cup salt |
| 4 | pounds. cucumbers, scrubbed and cut lengthwise |
| 7 | dill heads |
| 21 | whole peppercorns |

Heat the vinegar, water, and salt to the boiling point. Pack the cucumbers into 7 pint jars; add a head of dill and three peppercorns to each jar and fill to within half an inch of the top with the pickling liquid. Adjust the lids, seal, and process in a boiling water bath for 10 minutes.

*Note:* Two tablespoons of the dried seeds may be substituted for 1 head of dill. If you are fortunate enough to have the dill heads from the garden, place the beautiful circular formation against the side of the glass jar before arranging the cucumbers, for the look of prize-winning pickles at the county fair.

## Dilly-Beans

| | |
|---|---|
| 2 1/2 | cups vinegar |
| 2 1/2 | cups water |
| 1/4 | cup salt |
| Whole, raw string beans | |
| 2 | cloves garlic |
| 1/4 | teaspoon cayenne |

1      head dill

1/8   teaspoon pepper

Boil the water, vinegar, and salt. Vertically pack string beans in jars. Place garlic, cayenne, dill, and pepper in each jar. Cover with the vinegar solution; seal and put in hot water to process for 10 minutes. Keep for 2 weeks before eating.

### Old-Time Crock Pickles

"Measure enough water to cover cucumbers in a crock. For each quart of water use 2 tablespoons of salt, 2 cloves of garlic cut in half, 1/4 c. vinegar, plenty of dill (stalks, seeds, roots, everything) and 1 slice of rye bread. Put the pickles (scrubbed and pierced with a knife), dill, and rye bread in a crock. Put water in a pot, add salt, and when water comes to a boil, add vinegar. Bring back to a boil. Pour this boiling liquid over the pickles. Cover with a big dish, put a weight on the dish, and let it stand about five days, when they should be ready to eat."

*From an old family recipe book*

158

## Fennel
*(Foeniculum vulgare)*

Hardy annual, 3-5 feet

## Florence Fennel
*(Foeniculum vulgare, var. azoricum)*

Hardy annual, 4-6 feet

### How to Grow It

Sometimes perennial, sometimes biennial, sometimes annual, fennel will do whatever you want it to do. If fennel is cut back before it goes to seed, it will live on in the garden. Climate is another factor in the longevity of fennel.

Bluish-green, feathery foliage and yellow flowers provide an airy contrast in the herb or vegetable garden. Florence or sweet fennel, also called "finnochio," is frequently grown as a vegetable, its enlarged leaf base blanched and eaten and the seeds and leaves used as seasoning. Softly chartreuse and anise-flavored, the seeds have been gathered for centuries for making tea, in many different cultures, to quiet colicky babies.

There is a bronze form of fennel that is particularly attractive in herb bouquets as well as useful. Although not commonly available, it's worth watching for in seed catalogs.

### How to Use It

Fennel is one of the "meeting seeds" of olden days, when a colonial lady attending an all-day prayer meeting would carry a little packet of the aromatic seeds tied in a knot in the corner of her handkerchief for surreptitious nibbling during the endless sermons. I always thought this was because of its licoricelike flavor, but now I understand that it's because the fennel does indeed chase away the pangs of hunger.

The seeds have many other uses; as a natural seasoning for lamb, as "the fish herb," as an ingredient in curry, to enhance any pork roast or chops, and with apples.

"Eat fennel and grow thin," says one of the early herbalists, watching weight even then. We recently came upon an herbal weight-reducing preparation, FDA approved, which is one-half fennel seeds.

### Fennel Tea

Use 1/4 teaspoon of the seeds per cup; bruise them slightly and steep about 5 to 10 minutes in boiling water, or until the anise-flavored tea is to your liking. Serve with honey or lemon. Sweeten it if you're not counting calories.

### Christa Maria's Tea

| | |
|---|---|
| 1 | cup peppermint leaves, dried |
| 1 | cup chamomile flowers, dried |
| 1 | cup rose hips, dried and crushed |
| 1/2 | cup fennel seeds |
| 1/2 | cup linden blossoms, dried |

160

Thoroughly mix all ingredients and store in a tight container. To prepare tea, use one cup of the mixture to a teapot. Add 2 strings of rock candy to 6 to 8 cups of water and boil until rock candy is dissolved. Pour over the tea, and steep for 15 minutes. If additional sweetening is desired, use honey.

"Herbs should be gathered while in blossom. If left till they have gone to seed, the strength goes into the seed."

*American Frugal Housewife,* 1933

### Apple Fennel Cake

| | |
|---|---|
| 1/2 | cup butter |
| 1 c. | light brown sugar, packed |
| 1 | teaspoon allspice |
| 1/4 | teaspoon powdered cardamon |
| 1/2 | teaspoon fennel seed, thoroughly crushed |
| 1 | 20-ounce can apples, sliced for pie, drained |
| Red maraschino cherries, cut in half (optional) | |
| 1 | tablespoon lemon juice |
| 1 | package yellow cake mix |
| 1/4 | teaspoon mace |
| 1 | teaspoon vanilla |

Melt butter in a 13 x 9 inch baking pan. Combine brown sugar, allspice, cardamon, and fennel seed; mix well and pour over butter. Add apple slices and cherries, add lemon juice. To the cake mix, add mace and vanilla and prepare according to cake mix directions. Pour over fruit. Bake at 350° F for 50 to 55 minutes. Turn out on a tray. Serve warm or cold. Serves 18 to 20.

| | |
|---|---|
| **Garlic** | Perennial, 2 feet |
| *(Allium sativum)* | |
| **Giant Garlic** | Perennial, 4 feet |
| *(Allium scorodoprasum)* | |
| **Garlic Chives** | Perennial, 1 foot |
| *(Allium tuberosum)* | |

## How To Grow It

Pungent, important to many cultures, in cooking, and credited with unequaled medicinal powers, garlic is an herb to grow and use. Most people don't include it in their herb gardens, however, because seeds and plants are usually unavailable. Simply go to the closest supermarket and buy a bulb or two, the kind you use in cooking, from the produce department. Separate it, and each clove when planted will produce another bulb, which you can separate and use or plant again.

The culture is similar to that of onions; plant two inches deep and four inches apart in early spring. Plant the separated cloves blunt end down and pointed end facing upward. If you desire a good crop, give them full sun, good drainage, and a medium loam.

If you wish to fertilize, superphosphate (for good root growth), bone meal, and old manure are excellent. Dig as soon as the garlic tops are turning brown and cure in a dry spot before trimming the foliage prior to storage. You can also braid the tops into a chain of garlic bulbs, attractive to hang in your kitchen.

For those who do not like the full zest of garlic, I have a favorite trick. Plant a few of the cloves on top of pebbles and water kept in a decorative glass on a sunny windowsill. In a week or so you will have bright green tops to cut, the same as chives, to add to your cooking whenever garlic is suggested. This is a milder form of garlic seasoning, plus an easy houseplant. Once the bulb is exhausted, dispose of it and start new ones. It's easy to do and inexpensive.

162

Giant garlic, sometimes called "elephant garlic," is something to grow, harvest, and show to friends at the office. It's amazing. When properly grown, giant garlic will weigh a pound or more. Slightly milder than regular garlic, use it the same way in soups, stews, spaghetti sauce, and salads. It is a strong perennial. Dig some to use and divide and immediately replant the rest for next year's crop. If you do, you'll always have garlic in your garden. Incidentally, if planted in the spring of the year, giant garlic will not make the typical garlic clove segments and cannot be divided.

At the first sign of spring, wild garlic has, on the other hand, very small bulbs that can be dug and used as seasoning. They are, in my opinion, belligerently strong. I like them best added to vinegar for flavor—perhaps because in vinegar they can be diluted to a milder strength.

Garlic chives are neither garlic nor chives but a proper allium, from the same family. They grow like chives and taste like garlic and so are well named. A row of garlic chives is a field of starry blooms in August, constantly in motion, with the honeybees visiting every floret—a pretty picture on a hot summer day. Cut back the tops before they turn to seed or they will self-sow all over the garden. Harvest the garlic-flavored leaves any time you need them; use them in any recipe in which garlic is indicated.

Every third spring, propagate garlic chives by dividing the tuberous root systems or by growing.from seeds.

## How To Use It

When Secretary of State John Foster Dulles was dying from cancer, he received over five hundred letters describing various cures, many of them plant remedies; one of these was garlic. Many cultures, especially those located where garlic grows abundantly, eat garlic for health. Parsley, because of its chlorophyll content and breath-sweetening properties, is recommended as a follow-up. Garlic is also valuable in the garden, where it repels insects as it grows or when mixed into a potion and poured over infected plants.

163

If the aroma of garlic on your hands is not appealing to you, use a garlic press, a mortar and pestle, or smash it with the whack of a hammer on a wooden chopping block. Whole garlic can also be tossed into the cooking pot and then removed before the dish is served. Skewer it with a toothpick to make it easy to find.

Add garlic to anything you like—all Mediterranean dishes, chicken, lamb, salad dressings, cheese dishes, many vegetables (especially zucchini and tomatoes), soups, stews, and naturally, hot garlic bread, which is always a favorite. We find garlic and rosemary to be almost essential, often inseparable, seasonings.

### *Savory String Beans*

| | |
|---|---|
| 2 | cloves garlic |
| 2 | tablespoons olive oil, heated |
| 1 | quart string beans, cut in 1-inch pieces |
| 1 | teaspoon savory (or a few sprigs of the fresh) |

Add the garlic, speared on a toothpick, to the oil; add the string beans and savory and stir-fry for 10 minutes until crispy-tender. The beans will be bright green and delicious. Remove the garlic before serving.

# Germander
*(Teucrium chamaedrys)*

Perennial, 1 foot

## How To Grow It

Dark, glossy evergreen leaves on small, shrubby plants make this herb an effective hedge, or good for establishing a pattern for knot gardens. An excellent edging plant (second only to boxwood), germander takes well to clipping.

Sometimes called germander, frequently called *teucrium*, we call it a favorite. Twelve months of the year, *teucrium* provides an attractive design in our garden. In July it erupts into a show of pinky-lavender spikes, covered with honey bees busily plying their trade during the long, hot month. We clip this herb hard early in spring and then again just after blooming.

We have encountered no problems in growing *teucrium*. It tolerates ordinary soil and enjoys a sunny position. Although it can be grown from seed, its tendency to layer itself around each shrub makes rooted pieces suitable for instant bushy plants, once clipped. Cuttings also root easily, and the larger plants can be divided in spring or fall.

## How To Use It

Germander is a bitter herb, a fact I relearn with each clipping. As the leaves fly, I invariably get one into my mouth—an unpleasant experience. Once used medicinally, as a stimulant, a tonic, to combat jaundice, and for gout, today *teucrium* is an historical resident in the medicinal garden.

165

Germander is, however, primary to the bee garden. Left unclipped, the flower spikes continue to attract honey bees for most of the summer months. The lipped flowers are charming in all herbal bouquets.

## Horehound
### (*Marrubium vulgare*)

Perennial, 2 feet

### How To Grow It

Horehound (sometimes spelled "hoarhound") has escaped the herb garden and made itself at home along the sunny roadsides of California, where it now resides on wildflower lists. Horehound is far more temperamental in our garden, and we are still trying to determine what it wants—obviously not the climate of south-central Pennsylvania.

We have observed two plants side by side, one thriving and the other sulking, for no apparent reason. Yet we're very fond of this hairy, almost white-leaved perennial, so we persist in cultivating it. Horehound likes to be clipped; the cuttings are a harvest to put to good use.

The highly aromatic foliage is interspersed with tight clusters of flowers arranged in whorls along the long stems. It deserves an important position in the medicinal garden.

Propagate horehound by cuttings in spring or late summer, when evenings are cool and moist; or grow it from seeds, transplanted a foot apart. Good drainage, full sun, ordinary soil, and moisture are requirements.

## How To Use It

Horehound is a bitter herb, widely used in throat preparations. The leaves provide a tea for colds and coughs, asthma, and lung ailments. Sweeten the tea with honey.

### *Fine Horehound Candy*

"Take a large bunch of the herb horehound, as green and fresh as you can get it. Cut it up (leaves and stalks) with scissors. Scald twice a China teapot or covered pitcher, and then put into it the horehound, pressing it down hard with your hands. The pot should be about two-thirds full of the herb. Then fill it up with boiling water. Cover it closely, and put a small roll of soft paper into the mouth of the spout, to prevent any of the strength escaping with the steam. Set the pot close to the fire to infuse and keep it there till it comes to a hard boil. Then immediately take it away, and strain it into another vessel. Mix with the liquid sufficient powdered loaf sugar to make it very thick soft paste, then put over the fire and give it a boil, stirring and skimming it well. Take a shallow, square tin pan, grease it slightly with sweet oil, and put into it the candy as soon as it is well boiled, smoothing it over the surface with a wet knife blade. Then sift on some powdered sugar. Set it away to cool. When nearly congealed, score it into squares. It is good for colds, and coughs, and hoarseness."

From *Allen's Useful Companion*, 1879

167

# Hop
*(Humulus lupulus)*

Perennial vine, 6 feet and over

## How To Grow It

A vining plant with exceedingly rough, three-lobed leaves, hop needs support, or it will clamber over all the other plants in the garden. A six-foot or larger trellis of wire netting will work well; the hop will quickly cover the trellis to provide screening, shade, or background. A "hop-yard" is an enclosure especially designed to grow and contain hop. The best support is an arbor. (*Note*: Hop refers to the vine; hops refers to the strobiles or flowers.)

To start with seeds, you will need some special instructions. If planted outdoors in the fall, hop seeds will germinate in the spring. If planted indoors, the seeds should be soaked for twenty-four hours, then mixed with damp soil or sand and kept in the refrigerator for five or six weeks before being sown in flats. After danger of frost is over, the plants started indoors can be transplanted to the garden, two to three feet apart. Germination of hop is erratic and can take place over a period of two or three years—until you have the plants growing in your garden. Then they will "hop" all over the place unless you keep the vines cut back and well harvested.

Diseases rarely affect hop; but should blue mold or powdery mildew attack, cut back all diseased parts of the plants and burn those parts.

You will need both male and female vines to produce the cone-like collection of flowers (strobiles) that are used as the herb. Harvest the cones soon after they appear in early fall, finish drying them on screens away from light to retain the best color and flavor, and store them carefully in large, tightly-lidded containers. We use a tin lard can.

The Pennsylvania Dutch settlers brought this herb with them. It has since escaped their gardens, and you can sometimes find hop vines growing in the wild. Dig the roots in fall if you wish to have hops for your garden.


## How to Use It

Well known to brewers, hops are used in beer, ale, and porter. Hops are a fragrant addition to potpourri and also are used to dye materials. A small pillow stuffed with hops is a very old and successful remedy for insomnia, recorded to have worked for King George III. The same type of pillow, heated, was used by the good Pennsylvania German housewife to allay the pains of toothache. She called it a "hoppasock." Hops contain lupulin, which is sedative and tonic. A tea of hops, one teaspoon to a cup of boiling water, will make a good nightcap or remedy for headache.

To make a liquid to use in breadmaking, place a handful of hops in a quart of water, boil five minutes, then strain. The dough will rise faster and will have a delicious aroma and flavor.


### *Hops Shampoo*

| | |
|---|---|
| 1 | cup hops |
| 1 | quart water |
| 1 | pint castile shampoo |

Boil hops in water for 10 minutes and strain. Add the liquid to any good castile shampoo. It will give the hair great vitality.

### "Sommer Bier"

|     |                |
|-----|----------------|
| 1   | gallon hot water |
| 5   | pounds honey   |
| 1   | ounce hops     |
| 1/2 | cup brandy     |
| 1   | lemon, sliced  |

Combine water and honey; boil for 45 minutes, skimming frequently. Place hops in a muslin or cheesecloth bag and add to the water. Bring to a boil for 30 minutes or longer. Strain, pour into a large crock, and let stand for 4 days. Then pour liquid into a keg or larger jar; add brandy and sliced lemon. Close tightly until the Summer Beer is used.

—An Old Pennsylvania Dutch recipe from the
Wieand family collection

# Horseradish
*(Armoracia rusticana)*

Perennial, 3 feet

## How to Grow It

The first immigrants to this country brought this pungent root with them. The very hardy horseradish has since escaped those old gardens and can sometimes be found growing wild.

A strong perennial with a parsnip-like root with many branches, horseradish likes to stay in the same place year after year. It flowers profusely in spring. Horseradish should be propagated from root cuttings.

To do so, cut lengthwise slices of the root and plant them, large end up, in previously prepared soil or in the corners of the vegetable plot as they did in early gardens as a method of insect control. The young root cuttings can be harvested the following year, but leave part of the root in the patch to perpetuate the herb.

Horseradish enjoys good soil, a top dressing of manure in winter, and full sun. It will tolerate wet, clay soil.

## How To Use It

To grate it is to know it. Oh, that penetrating pungency! Gather horseradish only after the weather turns cold in October, dig through the winter and early spring, or as long as the ground can be broken. Grate horseradish and use it immediately or it will lose its pungency. First, wash and peel the fresh root, then grate it on a metal grater or in a food grinder, or, best of all, in a blender.

Brought here from Europe because it was essential to the colonists' high protein diet, horseradish made oversmoked or overripe meats palatable, promoted appetite, and stimulated digestion. Horseradish was considered good for rheumatism and palsy and also was used as a poultice.

Before the ground freezes solid, move a clump of horseradish from the garden to the cold frame or root cellar and store it in a box of damp sand so you may remove the horseradish pieces as you need them.

## Piquant Seasoning

| | |
|---|---|
| 4 | tablespoons grated horseradish |
| 1 | teaspoon sugar |
| 1 | teaspoon salt |
| 1/2 | teaspoon pepper |
| 2 | teaspoons good mustard |
| 3 | tablespoons cream (optional) |

Mix the herbs with sufficient vinegar to achieve the consistency of cream; then add the additional cream if desired. Serve hot on hot roast beef, cold on cold roast beef, or mix with ketchup to make a stimulating shrimp sauce.

# Lavender

| | |
|---|---|
| *(Lavandula augustifolia)* | Perennial, 1 to 3 feet |
| *(Lavandula latifolia)* | Perennial, 3 feet |
| *(Lavandula augustifolia var.* *'Hidecote')* | Perennial, 1 1/2 feet |
| *(Lavandula dentata)* | Perennial, tender, 2 feet |

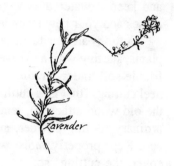

Lavender

## How to Grow It

Surely lavender was and is one of the world's most popular fragrances. The clean-smelling aroma permeates wherever it is used. To lay her linens away in fresh lavender every year earned the seventeenth century lady a high reputation for housewifery.

*Lavender augustifolia*, formerly called *officinalis* or *vera*, is English lavender, a compact, hardy, woody shrub with silvery leaves. The spiked variety, Latifolia, has dark gray leaves and grows considerably taller. 'Hidecote' is similar, with very dark flowers. *Dentata* is perennial, but tender in our climate, highly aromatic, and an excellent pot plant to grow for fragrance indoors. It will grow very well outdoors in California.

Seeds of lavender were among the first herbs brought to this country. Lavender grows readily from seed sown in March, in pots of good soil covered with glass until germination takes place in about two weeks. After germination, uncover the pot, place it in the strongest sun, and give a weak feeding of auxiliary food such as fish emulsion. The sturdy little plants will be ready for the garden by May.

Although lavender is a single-stemmed plant, it is possible to make occasional root divisions from a large healthy plant. Reach down to the base of the plant, below the soil line. Using a very sharp knife, cut away any side shoots that the plant has produced. A bit of root should be attached to each shoot. Plant a shoot in well-prepared soil, give it a glassful of liquid rooting hormone to reduce the shock, and keep it watered as well as shaded from hot sun until wilting ceases and your new lavender plant is on its own.

Cuttings are our favorite way to increase our supply of lavender plants, starting with a two-year-old plant. Prepare a bed of extremely friable soil under a rather dense shrub. Take four-inch or six-inch heel cuttings (that is, a cutting taken next to a main stem with a bit of the old wood attached), remove lower leaves, dip each cutting into ordinary rooting powder, and plunge the cuttings into the special bed. Kept properly moist with daily misting or by using a plastic cover, the cuttings should grow into new lavender plants in about two months.

Plant lavender in any part of the herb garden where its characteristic gray foliage and purple spikes will be featured. It demands perfect drainage and requires full sun—even a shading by an adjacent, overgrown plant can destroy it—and it prefers some protection from high winds. A fence, a rock, an evergreen shrub, or a close building can provide this protection.

We have lavender plants in our garden that vary in age and size. We keep starting vigorous young plants so that when we lose one lavender we can replace it with another. Unsuitable soil, bitterly cold winter, unfavorable position are only a few of the reasons, we imagine, why lavenders leave our garden. Love somehow doesn't seem to be enough to satisfy lavender. It grows only as long as it wishes to grow, bestowing its flowers and fragrance, its silvery stateliness on our herb garden with queenly largesse—or withdrawing it with no warning. We have learned to accept the

174

unpredictability of lavender and to keep a supply of replacement plants coming along at all times.

## How To Use It

As cosmetic, moth repellent, aromatic water, personal fragrance, lavender is everything sweet-smelling and feminine. Wherever it can be grown, it is gratefully harvested for its multitudinous, always fragrant uses.

### *Lavender Vinegar*

1/2     cup lavender flowers
1       pint white vinegar, heated

Steep lavender and vinegar together in a lidded jar in full sun for 2 weeks. Strain off the flowers, through muslin if necessary, and bottle for use. Wring out a cloth soaked in the lavender vinegar and place it on the brow while resting and relaxing. The fragrance of lavender dispels the vapors. Breathe deeply.

### *Old-Fashioned Lavender Scent Balls*

1/2     pound paraffin (or beeswax or
          even old candles)
1       dram oil of lavender

|     |                                   |
| --- | --------------------------------- |
| 2   | cups dried lavender flowers and leaves |
|     | Spices (optional)                 |
| 1/2 | ounce powdered orrisroot          |

Melt the paraffin; add oil of lavender, scented flowers and leaves, spices if you wish, and orris. When cool enough to handle, form into small balls. Allow them to dry thoroughly in the air before using them in drawers to perfume underwear, socks, and handkerchiefs. Smaller lavender balls can ornament your Christmas tree or be strung into a necklace.

Lavender

# Lemon Balm
*(Melissa officinalis)*

Perennial, 1 1/2 feet

## How To Grow It

Melissa is the easiest, most undemanding, and useful herb of all. Its chartreuse foliage enhances the herb garden, or any perennial border, and it's a joy to work amid its lemony fragrance. This pretty plant, about one and one-half feet tall, is a perennial with mint-like growth. It will tolerate semishade. Not at all fussy about soil or exposure or watering *Melissa* thrives undaunted. In fact, when treated too well with rich soil and fertilizers, the leaves will grow rank and lose much of their fragrance.

Two or three plants will produce an enormous yield, all of which you will want to use. Cut the plants back severely several times a year. Be sure to cut them before they go to flower and then, very quickly, to seed in June—unless, of course, you are cultivating *Melissa* for your honey crop. As Gerard says, "Bees are delighted with this herbe above others."

Hang the tied bunches to dry in a warm, airy place, out of direct light. After a few days, a delightful task is stripping the branches of the fragrant, lemony leaves.

Growing *Melissa* indoors for winter fragrance is not difficult. Lift seedling plants from the garden, or separate a large clump and plant it in good soil in a suitably sized pot. Place the pot outside until extremely cold weather has taken the tops. Then cut the plant back (about January), and bring it indoors to a bright window where it

177

will quickly send up the puckery, lemon-scented leaves you can use. The cold rest period is important to the health and vigor of the plant; tuck it in a corner of the refrigerator if necessary.


## How To Use It

Native to southern Europe, *Melissa* was used by the Romans, who advocated hot balm tea for nerves and fever. Our earliest colonists brought *Melissa* with them from Europe. They prized it for fragrance, flavoring, and medicine. Indeed, where else would they have gotten lemons?

Infuse the lemony tips of *Melissa* in a good grade of rubbing alcohol to make an invigorating rub for an invalid, or boil some into an infusion for a luxurious, relaxing, fragrant bath.

Added to tansy, southernwood, and santolina, in any quantity, dried lemon balm makes a fragrant, old-fashioned moth preventative. Sew it into flat pillows to lay between woolens. Bags of lemon balm under sofa cushions will also keep kitty from sharpening her claws on the furniture.

Bunches of lemon balm are a boon to outdoor living. If you entertain outside a great deal in the summertime, grow a row of this fragrant herb near your patio. You can rub the lemony leaves on your skin to repel gnats and other annoying flying insects while gardening or lolling in the sun. Whisks of lemon balm are handy at picnics for the same purpose. Also rub the picnic table with handfuls of the leaves before serving the food. It works rather like citronella to keep down the insect population.

Farmers once grew lemon balm in their pastures to help promote the flow of cows milk, also to strengthen the cows after calving. Rubbed down with the leaves, Bossy was free of flies while being milked.

If you have a fireplace in your home, the *Melissa* stems are also useful. After you have harvested the dried leaves, tie the stems together with yellow ribbons in small bunches to use as fragrant faggots when you start cheery winter fires.

Cooking with *Melissa* is a gourmet adventure. It may be used any way one would use a lemon except, of course, in slices. Fish, fruit, and vegetables, especially peas or spinach, benefit from a touch of *Melissa*. Garnishing with *Melissa* goes without saying—it's as attractive as it is fragrant.

### *Lemon Balm Cooler*

| | |
|---|---|
| 2 | cups lemon balm leaves, fresh or dried |
| 1 | quart boiling water |
| 1/2 | cup sugar |
| 1 | quart ginger ale |

Steep the leaves in water for 15 minutes, strain, add the sugar, and stir well. Add the ginger ale and serve with ice. Garnish with the fresh herb or lemon slices. For a special party, add lemon sherbet and stir until frothy.

### *Lemon Balm Tea*

Add 3 to 4 fresh or dried lemon balm leaves to each teacup before pouring your favorite regular tea. Delightful!

## *Melissa's Herb*

Every little girl named Melissa should cultivate lemon balm. She has a ready-made logo. Pressed leaves make lovely notepapers, all of the above uses and recipes are part of her image, and, of course, she should carry lemon balm in her wedding bouquet. Easy to grow, lemon balm plants should be Melissa's gift to everyone. It signifies "comfort."

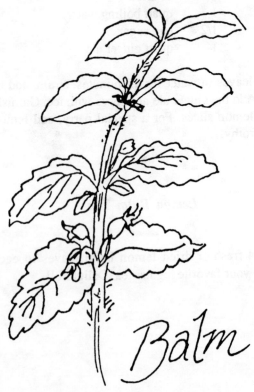

*Balm*

# Lemon Verbena
*(Aloysia triphylla)*

Tender perennial, 6 feet

## How To Grow It

If you like lemon, you'll adore lemon verbena, the lemoniest of them all. An old-fashioned favorite, it has always been grown for its outstanding fragrance. Not hardy north of Virginia, it is usually grown in tubs and moved about as a garden feature. We use our largest lemon verbena in the center of a small knot garden.

Native to South and Central America, lemon verbena was probably taken back to Europe by Spanish travelers before it was brought to the gardens of North America. In its native habitat, lemon verbena is a shrub which grows to ten feet. We keep ours clipped to about four feet, so it's easily moved indoors to a cool greenhouse every fall. As a houseplant, lemon verbena does very well in any sunny, cool window.

Although our plants have flowered occasionally, we have never seen the seeds of lemon verbena, even though we have inquired of many sources. Therefore, all our lemon verbenas are started from cuttings—an easy process. Firm four-inch woody pieces into good potting soil, using a rooting powder if you wish, and cover with plastic to retain moisture. New roots will form in about six weeks.

One word of caution about lemon verbena: it has a tendency to become dormant. When you move it indoors, when you transplant it to a larger pot, when you fertilize it, when you speak to it unkindly, it drops all its leaves. Please be assured that it is not dead, only sleeping. I don't know how many verbenas I tossed out before I learned this important fact. Since then, I have rarely lost a lemon verbena plant. Even if you do none of the above things to it, it will at some time, usually in early spring, become dormant for a period of one to two months. About the time you are convinced that it is dead, not dormant, you will note infinitesimal leaves, which quickly grow out into a fresh, new plant, green and lemony and beautiful. During

181

the dormant period, keep the plant moist (but not wet) and out of full sun, with just enough light and water to maintain life yet not support growth.

Outdoors, a small verbena cutting grows enough to fill a bushel basket in one short growing season. Harvest all the leaves you can and dry them for their many uses. Cut back the large plant before bringing it indoors in a pot for another winter.

## How To Use It

Housewives once sewed dried lemon verbena leaves into the darts of their Sunday dresses, replacing them when necessary—a fragrant, natural deodorant. You will recognize the highly aromatic fragrance as the popular lemon oil used in commercial soaps, candles, and spray sachets. The dried leaves contain great quantities of volatile oil and are important to potpourri.

One fresh leaf will influence a pot of ordinary tea, giving it a lemony lift. A tea made entirely of lemon verbena is said to be sedative; use one teaspoon per cup of boiling water, steep eight to ten minutes, and sweeten with honey. Use verbena in any drink, punch, or fruit cup. It is also nice in salads, with spinach, and in fish sauces. The dried leaves can be finely crumbled in a mortar and pestle, added to granulated sugar, and served on a tea tray. Lemon verbena is also a pretty garnish for desserts. In Victorian times fresh leaves were floated in finger bowls.

### *Lemon Tea*

When your lemon verbena plant goes dormant, gather the dried leaves and combine with lemon balm leaves, lemon grass, lemon thyme, lemon geranium and lemon peel, all dried and in any quantity you have available. Steep 1 teaspoon of the "herbal lemons" to a cup of boiling water for 5 minutes. Serve with honey.

# Lovage
*(Levisticum officinale)*

Perennial, 3 to 6 feet

## How to Grow

Sometimes called European celery, lovage looks like celery, tastes like celery, and smells like celery, but is different in a very important respect—we can grow it more easily in our gardens and gather the tasty leaves the better part of the year.

Lovage may be grown from fresh seeds, planted as soon as they ripen in August. These seeds will produce healthy young plants which will be ready for a gentle harvest the first year. Planted in the spring, lovage yields many savory leaves to enhance and garnish summer salads.

Plant lovage at three-foot intervals in full sun.. It is one of the few herbs that does not resent heavy clay and some dampness. Obviously, since it can grow up to four or five feet, it is most suitable as a background plant.

When your plant is sufficiently large, in three or four years, you can harvest part of the enormous root system. Return the numerous small offshoots to the garden, where they will renew your lovage planting.

I don't know where lovage acquired the name "love parsley," but I agree that it's a love of a plant—tasty, useful, and guaranteed to grow vigorously enough to make you feel all green thumbs.

## How To Use It

The leaves, seeds, and roots of lovage are used for flavoring foods. Fresh or dried, the leaves are best in soups, stews, creamed fish dishes, salads, and with tongue—any way that celery is used. They are also pretty as a garnish, especially under a portion of potato salad.

Stems are bitter except very early in the year, during April, when they are mounded up with soil to be blanched like celery. They can be stewed, creamed, or pureed for soup while young and tender. Being hollow, short lengths of the stem make unique drinking straws for tomato juice cocktail.

Lovage tea is made with leaves, seeds, or roots. The aromatic drink was popular centuries back as a home remedy, probably because it tasted so good. It was recommended for pleurisy, quinsy, and the ague, as a gargle, an eyewash, and to remove freckles.

Brew the tea by pouring a cup of boiling water over one teaspoon of roots, leaves, or seeds, and allow to steep until the flavor is to your satisfaction. Salted, this is a savory hot·brew. Sweeten it if you prefer.

The same infusion has unexpected merits when added to a tub of hot water. In days gone by, this was the ultimate in perfumed bathing, both soothing and invigorating.

### Lovage Dip

| | |
|---|---|
| 8 | ounces cream cheese |
| 3 | tablespoons cream |
| 1/2 | cup lovage leaves, finely chopped |
| 1 | tablespoon chopped chives |
| | Salt to taste |

Mix all ingredients together until creamy. Serve with chips or raw cauliflower. This is a favorite recipe.

### Love Bath Balls

| | |
|---|---|
| 7 | parts lavendar |
| 6 | parts rosemary |
| 5 | parts rose petals |
| 3 | parts lovage |
| 2 | parts lemon verbena |
| 1 | part each thyme, mint, sage, marjoram, and orris |

Mix all herbs (dried) and age together in lidded container 4-6 weeks. Cut 6" squares of fabric, place a heaping tablespoon in each, tie shut. Boil each bath ball in 1 quart water for 10 minutes. Add to hot bath water. Scrub with the ball. Think serene thoughts. Luxuriate!

lovage

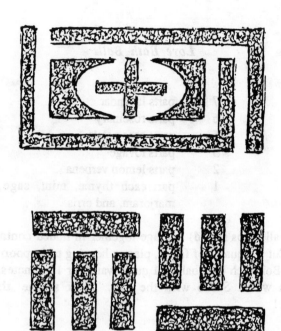

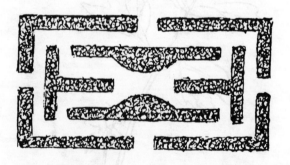

Various plans for your herb garden

# Marjoram/Oregano

| | |
|---|---|
| Common Marjoram | Perennial, 1 1/2 feet |
| *(Origanum vulgare)* | |
| or | |
| *Wild Marjoram* | |
| Sweet Marjoram | Tender perennial, 1 1/2 feet |
| *(Origanum majorana)* | |
| Pot Marjoram | Perennial, 2 feet |
| *(Origanum heracleoticum)* | |
| Dittany of Crete | Tender perennial, 1 foot |
| *(Origanum dictamnus)* | |

## How To Grow It

The confusion arising from the subject of marjoram and/or oregano causes horticulturists, herbalists, cooks, and plain dirt gardeners to take sides and do battle. How can any plant whose name means "joy of the mountains" cause such havoc?

I have made a hobby of purchasing all plants and seeds with the marjoram/oregano label and this has only heightened my confusion. The saddest disappointment is the oregano that invariably turns out to be the common wild marjoram. This perennial, *Origanum vulgare*, has little flavor, an oil that was once used medicinally, and a root system that invades like mint. In its favor are pretty lavender flowers on tall stems that dry beautifully for wreaths and winter bouquets. The creeping perennial root stock makes marjoram suitable for soil conservation in waste spaces, on steep banks, and along roadsides—or in its traditional, ancient location, on graves, where it may be mowed.

Sweet marjoram, sometimes called knotted marjoram because the flowers very cleverly convert into knotted seed heads, is again a pretty flower to harvest when dried. A tender perennial with a

187

pleasant flavor, sweet marjoram is worth planting in pots and bringing indoors for winter use.

Pot marjoram is a perennial with many pale mauve flowers, grayed leaves, and a distinct flavor. It grows in pots and is used in cooking pots—hence its name. It likes warm soil, a dry position, full sun, and annual replantings.

Dittany of Crete, another oregano houseplant north of Washington, D.C., is not easily acquired and is grown only from cuttings. Treasure it when you have it in your possession. The round, softly-felted leaves, gray and downy, grow well in California's climate. Highly aromatic, indigenous to the sunny dry hillsides of Crete, dittany should not be kept too wet. Give it direct sunlight and mist. Dittany is a most attractive hanging plant, and you may propagate it from cuttings made from the long shoots that hang over the sides of the container.

The oregano that I have grown as that herb is one foot tall with very grayed, small leaves and a strong flavor. It is not reliably hardy. I have shown it to people who have scoffed at my oregano and said, with disdain, "There is *no* oregano growing in this country," even though it is a seedling from a bundle of Greek oregano. In other words, it can't be grown here. What happens, I'm sure, is that, given the necessary adjustment to this climate and soil, the plant grows rank and comparatively flavorless, and loses its authority as the intensely flavorful imported dried oregano sold for pizza.

Sometimes the name marjoram or oregano depends entirely upon the country of origin and not the plant. 'Mexican oregano' is *Lippia graveolens*. Another plant of almost identical flavor and growth habit is *Coleus amboinicus;* there are also countless varieties of *Origanum vulgare* to add to the confusion.

Oregano, it seems, is a twentieth-century herb, being marketed widely only since World War II, when our soldiers were introduced to it abroad. Prior to that time it was almost foreign to herbal literature, which confines itself almost exclusively to the study of marjoram. Commercially, one is frequently intermixed or substituted for the other, depending upon supply and variety available. Plant or seasoning, marjoram/oregano can be said to be almost interchangeable.

This family of plants grows readily (except for dittany) from very small seeds sown early in spring or, to be sure you have the plant you want, from a root or stem cutting. Since seeds are slow and uncertain, we prefer the latter method. As Culpeper puts it, "Wild Marjoram has a root that creeps much underground, which continues a long time." Divided, this creeping root stock will create many plants faster than seeds.

## How To Use It

The Greeks grow marjoram/oregano on graves for the eternal bliss of the deceased; they crown their brides with it; call it "joy of the mountain"; and regard it as an essential seasoning. If you line up six different commercially marketed oreganos, the true Greek oregano will win the flavor test every time. Marjoram, you will find, is less pungent and less controversial.

Pillows stuffed with dried marjoram are recommended for those suffering from asthma, who should also try steaming cups of marjoram tea. Use either marjoram and/or oregano for strewing, to scour furniture, in sweet bags and "swete washing waters," as a dye made from the flowers, and in ale.

Cook with marjoram in soups, stews, chowders, on roast beef, lamb, fish, in all egg and cheese dishes, and with eggplant. Depending upon the source, it can be a strong flavoring, one to add with a light hand.

### *Girl Scout Pizza Rounds*

|  |  |
|---|---|
| 1 | box round crisp crackers |
| 1 | jar prepared spaghetti sauce |
| 1/2 | pound grated Parmesan cheese |
| 1/2 | cup oregano |

Place a dollop of spaghetti sauce on each cracker. Top with cheese and a pinch of oregano. Place on a cookie sheet to heat at 350⁰ F. for 10 to 15 minutes, or until cheese bubbles. Yield: enough for a troop.

*wild. Marjoram*

# Mint

### Apple Mint, Wooly
*(Mentha suaveolens)*
Perennial, 2 feet

### Spearmint
*(Mentha spicata)*
Perennial, 1 1/2 feet

### Peppermint
*(Mentha aquaticaXMentha spicata)*
Perennial, 3 feet

### Orange Mint
*(Mentha citrata)*
Perennial, 2 feet

### Corsican Mint
*(Mentha requienii)*
Perennial, 2 inches

## How To Grow It

Mint was one of the first plants brought to this country by the early settlers; it has made itself right at home here and has since escaped into the wilds where it is easily recognized by its familiar scent.

As Culpeper was wont to say in his seventeenth-century herbal, "These are so well known they need no description." Undoubtedly the most common herb, mint is also one of the oldest and most popular. It will grow almost anywhere and in abundance. It is one of the few herbs that will tolerate light shade; however, tree roots are not to its liking, so don't attempt to grow it under shade trees. Mint is also amenable to growing in damp situations—unusual for most herbs.

191

*Requienii* is the most pungent of the mints and yet the smallest. Called Corsican mint or jewel mint, it likes damp soil and some shade. It hugs the ground, like moss, so it is somewhat tolerant of being tread upon. The fragrance is delightful when crushed underfoot.

Apple mint has tall stems with rounded, softly-felted, gray leaves, and off-white flower spikes. Peppermint sports a tighter, more thrifty growth pattern with smooth, very pungent leaves on dark stems. Spearmint has smaller, pointed, slightly crinkled leaves on straight stems and is the one mint most often found growing wild. Orange mint is a very pretty, smooth-leaved plant with a decidedly citrus mint flavor. It is especially attractive in fall when the leaves turn a deep russet.

There are many other varieties of mint, all distinguished by their aromatic leaves and invasive growth habits. We grow curly mint, variegated spearmint, black peppermint, pineapple mint, and a hybrid of *Mentha citrata*, "eau de cologne" mint. Besides these, there are mountain mints, pennyroyals, bergamots, and enough species, varieties, and hybrids of the family *Mentha* to fill an entire book.

Two words of caution in the growing of mints. First, do not plant more than one kind of mint in a patch, lest they become hopelessly entangled. Second, be ruthless in the maintenance and control of your mint patches. They will send out long root runners and need to be held in check by drastic measures.

You may be able to control mint plants by planting them in large, old, bottomless tubs, metal or plastic, sunk into the ground to rim level. Dig or pull the mint out as you would any other unwanted plant when it exceeds its boundaries. The thinnings can be used or shared with others.

Propagate mint by root divisions, cuttings, or seeds. Pieces of mint used in bouquets will sometimes root in water. *Note*: Mint grown from seed may produce crossed progeny. For best results, purchase plants from reliable sources and propagate mints vegetatively.

## How To Use It

If you have a mint plant, you have a lot of mint. Mint is generously productive, one of our favorite herbs and also, thank goodness, one of the most useful herbs. Reap your fragrant, minty harvest and use every bit of it, if in no other way than as "a good posie for students to oft smell."

### *Mint Tea*

Fresh or dried, mint makes an excellent tea. Add 1 tablespoon of the fresh herb (1 teaspoon of the dried) per cup of boiling water. Allow the tea to steep for 7 to 10 minutes.

When you have your own fresh mint available, cut a quantity and strip the stems from bottom to top with your hand. Fill a glass or enamel pitcher with the fallen leaves and pour boiling water over them. Steep 10 to 20 minutes; dilute with water or regular tea to the strength desired. This makes a refreshing mint tea that can be served hot or iced and is said to aid the digestion, clear the head, and remedy hiccoughs. Besides, it's delicious.

### *Candied Mint Leaves*

| | |
|---|---|
| 1 | egg white |
| Green food coloring | |
| 2 | cups granulated sugar |
| 48 | large, whole mint leaves |

193

Whip the egg white until just frothy; add a few drops of green food coloring. Add another few drops of green coloring to the sugar, mix thoroughly, and dry on a cookie sheet for an hour or two. Wash the leaves; pat fairly dry. Dip the leaves into the egg white; lay aside on waxed paper. Sift the pale green sugar over the leaves, turning the leaves so that both sides are covered. If you wait a few seconds between each step of dipping and sugaring, the egg and sugar will form a better bond with the leaves. Allow the leaves to dry thoroughly for two weeks before packing them in tins for later use or gift-giving.

## Minted Peas And Carrots

This is a recipe designed to make frozen peas taste as if they have been freshly harvested. Add a few mint leaves to a box of frozen peas during the regular cooking process. Butter and serve.

Carrots, fresh or frozen, cooked in pineapple juice with mint become true company fare. Serve the peas one day, the carrots the next, and combine the leftovers into a superb dish by thickening with cornstarch.

## Mint Sugar

Put 4 to 6 mint leaves and a cup of sugar in the blender; add a few drops of green food coloring. Blend on high until well blended. Dry the sugar overnight on a cookie sheet before storing for later use on cookies and grapefruit and in tea; or roll little green grapes in mint sugar for an attractive, delicious garnish.

## Nancy's Mint Cookies

| | |
|---|---|
| 1 | cup butter |
| 1/2 | cup sugar |
| 1/4 | teaspoon salt |
| 1 | teaspoon peppermint extract |
| 2 | tablespoons crushed, dried mint leaves |
| 2 | cups flour |

Cream butter and sugar. Add salt, extract, mint leaves, and flour. Mix thoroughly. Chill the dough. Form 1-inch balls and roll in sugar. Press with your thumb. Bake at 350⁰ F. for 12 to 15 minutes. Makes 3 dozen. For a variation, top with chocolate kisses before baking.

## Mint Essence

Here is a practical way to store your mint for wintertime use. Add 4 cups of fresh peppermint leaves to 1 cup sugar and 1 cup water. Simmer over low heat until the mixture is reduced by half. Strain, bottle, and seal.

## Mint Vinegar

Harvest as many mint tops as you have, wash them, and cram them into a crock or large jar. Pour hot, not boiling, white vinegar over them and let stand 14 days in full sun. Strain and bottle. A few drops of green food coloring can be added. This delicious vinegar can be used on fruit salads, thickened as a sauce to go with lamb, or sweetened and thickened to serve over ice cream. The leaves can also be preserved in a jar with some of the vinegar.

### Mint Cordial

Pick 2 quarts of spearmint leaves, preferably during the month of May. Pour 2 quarts of rectified spirits or proof brandy over them and let them draw for 48 hours.

Strain the liquor from the leaves. Dissolve 3 pounds of clear, white rock candy in the cordial and bottle it.

### Mint Jelly

| | |
|---|---|
| 1/2 | cup dried mint (or 1 cup fresh) |
| 1 | cup boiling water |
| 3 | cups sugar |
| 2 | tablespoons lemon juice |
| 1/2 | bottle pectin |

Place the mint in a large saucepan. Pour the boiling water over the mint, cover, and let stand 1/2 hour or until it is very minty. Strain the mixture, returning the liquid to the saucepan. Add the sugar and lemon juice to the mixture and boil for several minutes. Add the pectin; boil another minute. Add a few drops of green food coloring, if desired. Pour into small glasses; cover with paraffin and label. (Receipe may be doubled.)

# Nasturtium
## (*Tropaeolum majus*)

Annual, 1 foot

## How to Grow It

Nasturtiums are herbs of the first order, pretty in the herb garden or any garden, and very tasty as a slightly hot seasoning. Garden records show that Thomas Jefferson grew nasturtiums at Monticello—"in 35 little hills," he instructed his gardener. They were used for salads because they were available after radishes had gone to seed.

Anyone who has grown nasturtiums will tell you they are ridiculously easy to grow. They need full sun and poor soil. Overfertilizing will cause an excess of foliage. Since both foliage and flowers are edible, don't deny yourself the touch of brilliance provided by rich shades of red, orange, and yellow nasturtium blossoms in your garden and in your cuisine.

The one problem encountered in growing nasturtiums is their vulnerability to aphids. We do several things about this; plant the nasturtiums in different parts of the garden each year; and gently water them from a sprinkling can containing water and some old cigar butts steeped overnight—a non-poisonous spray. We also tried purchasing a pint of lady bugs in the hope they would make themselves welcome in a patch of aphid-infested nasturtiums, but they promptly "flew away home." The positive side of this story is that aphids attracted to nasturtiums leave other plants alone.

Nasturtiums provide a bonus as houseplants. If you have a very sunny window, you can take cuttings from your nasturtium plants, root them in water, and pot them to grow indoors for colorful, zesty seasonings during the winter months. Seeds germinate faster if soaked overnight in water. They are very satisfying to small children, who love to poke the seeds into pots of soil and watch them grown.

197

# How To Use It

As soon as the plump seeds sprout, you can begin harvesting nasturtium leaves to use to season salad. Rolled in slices of thin, white, buttered bread, the peppery leaves make delicious, attractive sandwiches which taste very much like watercress (a cousin) sandwiches.

John Randolph of Williamsburg thought "the flower is superior to a radish in flavor." President Eisenhower, who enjoyed cooking, added about a tablespoon of nasturtium leaves and stems, finely chopped, near the end of cooking his famous vegetable soup.

If you like to stir up conversation when you entertain, use the bright blooms as a glorious garnish for green applesauce. They raise that simple dish far above the ordinary.

Nasturtiums are also beneficial to other plants: grown in orchards and vegetable gardens they serve as both crop and insecticide. Always plant them near radishes, potatoes, or squash.

### *Pickled Nasturtium Seeds*

Soak the seed in salt water for 3 days, stirring occasionally. Heat together 1 quart white wine, 6 shallots, 1 tablespoon horseradish, and a pinch of salt, pepper, cloves, mace, and nutmeg. Cover the seeds and bottle for later use as capers.

Adapted from *The Compleat Housewife*, 1728

### *Stuffed Nasturtium Blossoms*

1        cup tuna fish, cut small

| 1 | tablespoon parsley, minced |
| 2 | tablespoons sweet pickle relish |
| 1/4 | cup pecans, cut |
| 4 | tablespoons mayonnaise |
| 24 | large nasturtium flowers, washed |

Combine all ingredients except nasturtiums. Carefully fill each blossom with the mixture. Arrange the colorful salads on a platter of lettuce or nasturtium leaves. They look smashing.

### *Nasturtium Sauce*

| 1 | teaspoon salt |
| 1 | quart vinegar |
| 1/2 | teaspoon cayenne |
| 8 | shallots, well bruised |
| 1 | quart nasturtium blossoms |

Simmer all ingredients except the flowers for 10 minutes. Pour hot vinegar mixture over the blossoms and cover. Set aside for 2 months. Strain and bottle, Use on salads or to make sauces.

### *Nasturtium Spray*

Take the highly aromatic leaves, stems, and flowers of nasturtiums; add an equal amount of boiled water and infuse overnight. Strain and pour into a sprinkling can; fill with water and pour on infested plants. This is especially good against whiteflies in the greenhouse, wooly aphids on apple trees, squash bugs, potato bugs, and beetles on radishes.

## Onion, Garden
*(Allium cepa)*

Grown as annuals, 18 inches

## Onion, Top Setting
*(Allium cepa viviparum)*

Grown as biennials, 18 inches

## How To Grow It

My horticultural dictionary lists eighty-four botanical varieties of onions, not including chives, leeks, garlic, shallots, and the ornamental onions. Alliums are a large family of honest herbs. As Culpeper puts it, "This plant is so well known that it need no description."

Professional onion growers agree that to raise these plants from seed would be doing it the hard way. A harvest of the succulent bulbs will take an endlessly long growing season. Onion sets purchased in early spring establish a head start on your onion harvest. Planted by the first day of spring, they should be well grown and harvested by July. Braid the tops onto a piece of rope, to hang in storage for winter use.

Plant the sets close to the soil's surface, in open, sunny areas—the vegetable garden or in the back of the herb garden. For a successful crop, enrich the soil; old manure is best.

Top-setting onions (also known as winter onion, perennial onion, Egyptian onion, or tree onion) are great fun to have in the herb garden. Truly unique, they are always conversation pieces—and perennial, if you don't dig them for use. Once you have these horticultural curiosities, you'll never be without them.

Instead of producing the usual onion flower balls, top-setting onions bypass flowers and seed production and make bulblets on top of tall, hollow stalks. Some of the bulblets can be planted, some eaten. They live and grow over the winter. Tops, hollow young stalks, and roots are edible. Pickle the top onions; the hollow stalks make perfect onion rings; chop the root as you would any other onion. When they are topped with the little bulbs, sometimes with a second tier of bulblets, these onions make attractive flower arrangements.

## How To Use It

Medicinally, onions are nature's cure-all for poor appetite, coughs, colds, croup, worms in children, and pneumonia, as antiseptic, and for scalds, ear noises, and skin blemishes. Worshiped by ancient Egyptians, who were not the first to respect its virtues, the onion has traveled with men and women on all explorations and conquests.

To try using the onion for colds, wrap a large one, laced with honey, in foil and bake until tender—an hour or two; bake the onion with butter and savory herbs—some basil, thyme, and oregano—and treat your family to a superb vegetable.

There is hardly a dish that is not improved by onions, the universally favorite seasoning. Use them generously, raw or sautéed. Use them as vegetables—creamed, stuffed, or in the justly famous onion soup.

### Onion Soup

| | |
|---|---|
| 1/2 | pound onions. thinly sliced |
| 1/4 | pound butter |
| 2 | tablespoons flour |
| 2 | quarts consommé |

Sauté the onions in butter until golden; add flour and brown slightly; add consommé slowly, while stirring. Simmer 1/2 hour. Strain, if you like, and serve. In each steaming bowl, float a piece of toast sprinkled with Parmesan cheese and thyme, and broiled until bubbly, for 2 minutes.

| Parsley, Curly | Biennial, 10 inches |
| *(Petroselinum crispum)* | |
| Parsley, Plain | Biennial, 12 inches |
| *(Petroselinum crispum var.* | |
| *neapolitanum)* | |
| Parsley, Turnip-Rooted | Biennial, 15 inches |
| *(Petroselinum crispum var.* | |
| *tuberosum)* | |

## How To Grow It

Parsley seeds are notoriously hard to germinate, sometimes taking up to three weeks. It is possible to speed the process by soaking the seeds in warm water for several hours or overnight. If you are starting them indoors, another good trick is to heat the bottom of the seed pan by placing it on a radiator or a heating pad or over a furnace.

Parsley is a biennial and must be planted every year to ensure a continual supply. Because it lives over at least one winter, parsley can be picked for a twelve-month period if it is given a protective covering. The frame of a bottomless box covered with heavy plastic or an old window sash is ideal for growing parsley through the winter months.

Parsley is an excellent edging plant in the herb garden, agreeable as a houseplant in a very sunny window, and graceful in a decorative hanging pot in your kitchen window. Parsley is not sheared like other herbs; rather, it is better to pick only the outer leaves so that new leaves will continue to grow from the central crown.

Plain, or Italian, parsley has the most flavor. Curled parsley is decorative; use it raw or fresh as a garnish. Turnip-rooted parsley is popular in Europe, where the tops, as well as the parsnip-like roots, are used to flavor soups and as a vegetable.

How To Use It

The roots, seeds, and vivid green leaves are used generously as a flavoring in almost everything: soups (especially chicken), stews, salads, eggs, and in melted butter over boiled potatoes. In ancient times, parsley was used in victory garlands and as a strewing herb for Roman banquets, which points up the effectiveness of abundant chlorophyll in parsley for absorbing odors. Parsley contains three times as much vitamin C as oranges and is also rich in vitamin A and iron, which explains its value as a medicinal tea herb. Parsley tea is taken as a mild diuretic and for rheumatism or colds and is used on the hair to discourage baldness, or so it is said. One teaspoon of dried parsley equals two sprigs of the fresh.

## *Three Ways To Preserve Parsley*

1. Dry the curled tops in the oven, one layer deep on a baking sheet, for 20 minutes at 150° F. When chip-dry, store the tops in dark, tightly-lidded jars. Label and date. (Hanging parsley to dry can be disappointing, as parsley usually loses its color and, therefore, its flavor.)
2. Plunge it into ice water before freezing it on a cookie sheet. After parsley is quick-frozen, pack it into freezer containers for later use. This is the best way to preserve parsley.
3. The old-fashioned method is to alternate layers of chopped parsley tops and coarse salt in crocks or jars. Seal with waxed paper and a tight lid; store in a cool place. Use as needed, but delete salt from the recipe.

### Parsley Tea

Use 1 teaspoon of the dried herb or a larger quantity of the fresh.
Pour boiling water over the parsley and allow it to steep for 10
minutes, or until desired strength is achieved. Sweeten with honey, if
you like, or add lemon.

### French-Fried Parsley

Wash and drain the curly tops of parsley. Plunge them into
heated deep fat for a few seconds. Serve immediately as a garnish or
as an appetizer.

### Parsley Mayonnaise

| | |
|---|---|
| 1 | cup parsley |
| 2 | tablespoons vinegar |
| 2 | cups mayonnaise |

Blend the parsley and vinegar together or crush them in your
mortar and pestle. Add to the mayonnaise and serve as a green
dressing with salads and vegetables.

### Lemon-Parsley Sauce

1/2      cup parsley, stems and all
1        medium onion
1        clove garlic
1/2      teaspoon salt
The juice of 1 lemon
1/2      cup softened butter

Blend the parsley, onion, and garlic in a mortar with pestle until smooth (or use your blender). Add the salt and lemon juice. Mix together with the butter. Brush on fish before broiling.

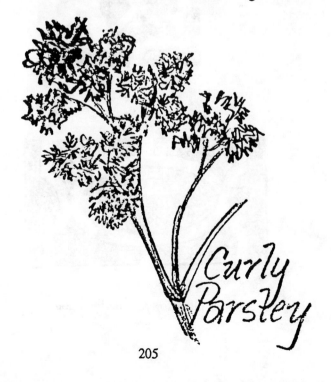

Curly Parsley

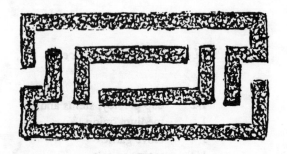

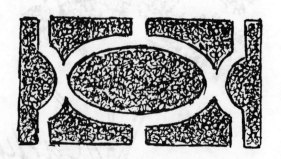

Various plans for your herb garden

## Pennyroyal, English
*(Mentha pulegium)*

Perennial, 6 inches

## Pennyroyal, American
*(Hedeoma pulegiodes)*

Annual, 1 foot

### How To Grow It

Both pennyroyals have a cool, clean, refreshingly minty aroma and identical uses. English pennyroyal is a perennial and grows very low, forming flat mats close to the ground. The American, or mock pennyroyal, is an annual, which grows about a foot tall and is found in clumps along roadsides and the fringes of woodland.

Both pennyroyals are easily grown from seed, the English accepting more moisture than our native, which prefers a dry situation. English pennyroyal, a true mint, is a perennial but hardy only in mild climates. We have rarely overwintered it successfully except in the greenhouse where, like all mints, it needs to be "rested" in an unheated corner. As it does in the wild, American pennyroyal in the garden reseeds itself; the English pennyroyal will need to be replanted every year if it is not hardy where you live.

### How To Use It

Insect repellent, herbal tea, water purifier, wildflower, charm against witches—pennyroyal is an herb of many virtues. The first colonists greeted the native American pennyroyal as an old friend, a welcome reminder of home. In settlers' homes, bunches of pennyroyal hung in the attic for a purpose—a hot cup of tea at any time, but especially before retiring on days after working outside in cold, wet weather. "A comforting infusion for the poor," pennyroyal was believed to help ward off illness.

Dried pennyroyal was also stuffed into mats to keep down vermin, and today's housepets will benefit greatly from pennyroyal bedding for the same reason. Stable boys slept on mattresses of this herb, a custom that dates back to biblical times, when pennyroyal, it is assumed, was one of the herbs used to line Christ's manger in Bethlehem. (See Index—"Holy Hay.")

Today, pennyroyal oil sprinkled around the barn or Fido's bed will dispel fleas, and a dab behind Kitty's ears will give her relief from these pests, too. But to free your pet of fleas and ticks, give it a rubdown of pennyroyal leaves steeped in water. A gardener working outside will find that rubbing the pungent leaves on exposed skin is an equally useful insect repellent for humans.

During those first endless voyages across the ocean, the water supply aboard ship was treated with pennyroyal because it was believed to purify water. The great herbalist Gerard wrote, "If you have Pennyroyale in great quantity, dry and cast it into corrupt water, it helpeth it much, neither will it hurt them that drink thereof."

### Pennyroyal Tea

One teaspoon per cup of boiling water, steeped 5 minutes or more. Sweeten if desired. Enjoy! Drink to relieve headaches, colds, fever, and nervousness. *Caution*: Pennyroyal is known to be a abortant. This tea should be avoided during pregnancy.

# Rosemary
*(Rosmarinus officinalis)*

Tender perennial, 1 to 6 feet

## How to Grow It

An ancient herb, rich in legend and history, beloved symbol of love and friendship, rosemary is considered the herb of Christmas, weddings, and also funerals. Said "to grow well where the mistress is master," perhaps explains why it seems difficult to grow. I'd say it grows very well indeed, so long as it remains in one place, outdoors.

A tender perennial, native to warm Mediterranean countries, rosemary flourishes in the sunny garden all summer. Grow it in a well-drained spot in the foreground or background—the choice depending upon the size or whether you wish to keep it clipped—and give it an occasional bit of lime.

Rosemary can be grown easily from seeds, which we do every March, or purchased as an established plant. Once you have it growing for you, it is easy to take cuttings and start as many plants as you want. Take three-inch to five-inch cuttings of not-too-new growth. Scrape the bottom inch of the stems slightly, dip them into a rooting powder, then firm them into good, humus-rich soil under the protective shade of an overgrown shrub. Cover them with a large jar and leave them to their own devices for four or five weeks. The big jar will allow the defenseless little cuttings to transpire without losing moisture. As the moisture condenses against the sides of the jar, the drops of water return to the earth around the cuttings and keep them going until new roots are formed. Water the cuttings during dry spells, of course.

Outdoors, rosemary is no problem, growing along at a fair rate in our area and bursting its seams farther south. Around Virginia, it is hardy. Plants started from seed sown in March will be a foot and a half tall by the end of the summer, when, in northern gardens, they are potted to bring indoors.

209

As a houseplant, rosemary prefers a small pot with perfect drainage and a sunny situation in a fairly cool room. Cool sun is sometimes difficult to arrange. Keep it misted for added humidity and pinch the tips to promote bushy growth. When the days begin to lengthen, occasionally feed it with a mild fertilizer. Do *not* overwater.

## How To Use It

There are several varieties of rosemary—white-flowered, pine-scented, purple-flowered, and even a prostrate form, which is slower growing and most attractive, especially in hanging baskets. All of these are similar to *officinalis* in that they have short, needle-like leaves, evergreen with a distinctly pine-like scent, and lipped flowers several times a year. The varieties have identical uses

Since rosemary is an ancient herb associated with many cultures, there are more ways to use it than can be covered here. In general, use rosemary liberally when cooking meats, fish, poultry, soups, salads, vegetables, biscuits, dumplings, eggs, appetizers, and, particularly, Mediterranean dishes in which rosemary is indispensable.

You can crush it between your fingers to release the essential oil and flavor, or powder it in a mortar with pestle, if you prefer. Here are a few special tricks: rosemary in mashed potatoes or cauliflower is vastly different and makes them better; rosemary is especially compatible with eggplant; rosemary and red beets are surprisingly harmonious; and four leaves of rosemary in chicken salad that stands for several hours before serving has an undefinably different flavor.

Rosemary isn't exactly a quiet herb; use it with care until you and your family have acquired the necessary taste for it. Then there is no need for caution.

*Officinalis* refers to the fact that this variety is used medicinally. Although the early herbalists credit rosemary with all manner of miraculous powers, much of its importance as a medicinal plant has faded. The pendulum, however, always swings and perhaps this may change. As recently as the early 1900s an English physician wrote, "Rosemary wine, taken in small quantities, acts as a quieting cordial." Another herbal directs one to "Boyle the leaves in white wine and washe thy face therewith and thy browes and thou shalt have a fair face." That's worth a try.

In countries where rosemary grows quite large, the wood is used to make small musical instruments and fine tools. The real value of the wood, however, is far greater, as revealed in another of my favorite quotes: "Make thee a box of the wood of rosemary and smell to it and it shall preserve thy youth." Every time I lose a rosemary plant, I save the wood to make my box!

When you have enough rosemary growing in your garden, you can braid it into garlands as was done in days of old and use it for protection against witchcraft. More likely, you will gather little bunches and dry them to use in your cooking. Hardly another herb is as versatile.

Cosmetically, rosemary has an honorable history. Boil the leaves in water for ten minutes, strain, and add to your tub for a soothing, relaxing bath, good for the nerves and muscles. Rosemary has been associated with the head and hair for centuries, so the same boiled leaves can be added to your favorite shampoo to make a marvelous hair conditioner.

The most famous cosmetic of all is Budapest Water, a queen's secret. Hungarian women are noted for their beautiful complexions. According to legend, Queen Elizabeth of Hungary, a famous beauty, was so attractive at the age of seventy that she inspired a young man of twenty-six with "a burning passion." The following recipe is her secret beauty bath, which may also be diluted to make a luxurious toilet water.

211

## Budapest Water

| | |
|---|---|
| 4 | ounces rosemary leaves |
| 1 | cup mint leaves |
| 1 | cup lemon balm |
| 2 | cups rosewater |
| 1 | pint alcohol |
| Peel of fresh lemon | |
| Peel of fresh orange | |

Place all herbs, dried (or double amounts if fresh from your garden), into a large jar and pour the liquids over them. Let the mixture stand for a month in a warm place, then strain and filter. Budapest Water can be used at your own risk as a cologne or in your bath.

## Rosemary Jelly

| | |
|---|---|
| 1 | cup rosemary leaves (1/2 cup dried) |
| 2 | cups water |
| 1/2 | cup vinegar |
| 6 1/2 | cups sugar |
| 1 | bottle pectin |

Bruise the leaves thoroughly in a mortar and pestle; move to a saucepan and add all ingredients except pectin. Bring to a rolling boil; boil for 2 minutes; add pectin. Boil 1 minute longer. Strain through colander and cloth. Pour into a jar and seal with paraffin at once.

212

## Rosemary Tea

| | |
|---|---|
| 4 | cups boiling water |
| 1/4 | cup rosemary |
| 2 | tea bags |
| 2 | cups sugar |
| 1 | cup water |
| 1 3/4 | cup lemon juice |
| 1 | gallon water |

Add boiling water to rosemary and tea bags; steep 10 minutes; strain. Boil the sugar and cup of water into a simple syrup; when cool, add lemon juice. Add syrup to rosemary base and mix. Add mixture to one gallon of water in an enamel pot. Heat; but do not boil. Serve tea hot or on ice with sliced orange and sprigs of rosemary. Makes 1 1/2 gallons.

## To Grow Hair

| | |
|---|---|
| 1 | tablespoon olive oil |
| 1 | tablespoon rosemary oil |
| 1 | tablespoon lemon grass oil |

Mix all ingredients and rub on the roots of hair at night.

Old recipe, 1859

Note: Alas, this will not grow hair where there is none.

### Merry Sherry

| 1 | gallon dry sherry |
| 10 | 6-inch sprigs fresh rosemary |
| 4 | ounces honey |

Steep all ingredients for 3 days. Remove rosemary. Chill and serve at very special affairs with a decorative sprig of rosemary in the decanter. "It shall keep thee youngly."

*"As for Rosemary, I lette it run all over my garden walls, not onlie because my bees love it, but because it is the herb sacred to remembrance and to friendship, whence a sprig of it hath a dumb language."*

**Sir Thomas More**

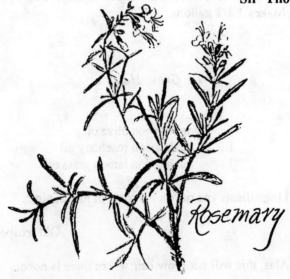

Rosemary

# Rue
*(Ruta graveolens)*

Perennial, 2 feet

## How To Grow It

Shakespeare's highly aromatic "herb of grace" is striking in the garden; plant it for accent in a sunny, well-drained location and cut large bouquets for indoors. It can be an unpredictable perennial, however, so when it leaves your garden, replace it quickly by keeping a supply of cuttings coming along in your shaded rooting bed.

The variety *graveolens* comes from seeds. It is a more floriferous, taller, greenish-blue than the hybrid variety, "Blue Beauty," which is propagated only from cuttings, and has the most brilliant blue foliage of all perennials. When the sun strikes this opalescent beauty, everyone stops to admire.

Cut *graveolens* in early spring for bushy, compact growth; later, cut only enough to keep it well shaped—or for bouquets. For cuttings, use only young growth, which will root in less than a month.

## How To Use It

Symbol of repentance, rue was used in the early church to sprinkle holy water; its well-branched structure and compound leaflets were well-suited to this purpose.

Rue has a catalog of medicinal benefits. It is said to preserve sight, work against epilepsy, and produce a tea for rheumatism and almost all other aches and pains—earache, stomachache, backache, leg ache, eye ache, the ague, and gout. It is an antidote for poisons and comforting on the bites of bees, wasps, spiders, and serpents. There's more!

Rue has a strong, clean fragrance, reminiscent of honest-to-goodness, old-fashioned soap. It was once considered useful as a strewing herb for warding off contagion, fleas, and insects. Judges carried sprigs of rue to ward off jail fever and as protection against pestilences in the air. These antiseptic qualities were once put to use by four loathsome thieves, who made a brew of rue to rub on themselves for protection from the great plague of Marseilles, while they plundered the homes of the victims.

Rue makes a pungent, aromatic vinegar. This should be diluted and used very sparingly on salads, or, better still, rub the vinegar on yourself while you are working in the garden.

### Vinegar Of The Four Thieves

| | |
|---|---|
| 3/4 | cup mint leaves |
| 1/4 | cup rosemary leaves |
| 2 | tablespoons sage |
| 1/2 | ounce each cloves, cinnamon, pepper, allspice, mustard seed |
| 1 | tablespoon rue |
| 1 | tablespoon salt |
| 2 | cloves garlic |
| 2 | tablespoons tarragon |
| 1 | bay leaf |

Combine all of the above ingredients; add 1 quart red wine vinegar, heated almost to boiling. Place vinegar mixture in a covered jar for 2 weeks, rolling it gently each day. Strain through a double thickness of cloth; bottle. All leaves used in this recipe are green; reduce each ingredient by 1/2 if dried herbs are used.

**Note:** On extremely hot humid days, rue can cause a sudden troublesome dermatitis. Avoid contact on such days.

# Saffron
*(Crocus sativus)*

Perennial bulb, 6 to 8 inches

## How To Grow It

October brings new interest into the herb garden with the blooming of saffron. Equal in value to gold, the bright reddish-orange harvest must be gathered in fall, when Pennsylvania German housewives pick the colorful stigmas from century-old patches. The stigmas are then dried and stored in wooden saffron boxes, now heirlooms, for making famous saffron breads and potpies.

Plant the bulbs in fall but be forewarned—the spot must be well marked or you will lose them between the planting and the first harvest the following fall. I lost my first two plantings, so I know how easily this can happen. They can be pulled up with weeds in the spring or overplanted with petunias. Mark the spot.

Slender, grass-like leaves will appear in spring and then disappear with no further sign of life until the lovely lavender crocus flowers appear like magic the following fall, "naked and without stalks." The hardy little bulbs then rest quietly through the long winter. They can be lifted and divided every few years to increase your planting.

Do not confuse *Crocus sativus* with the larger *Colchicum*, sometimes called autumn crocus because it blooms at the same time. The *Colchicum* is something else again—a drug plant used in the treatment of gout and definitely not to be used in cooking or, for that matter, as a home remedy. Identification is easy since *Colchicum* has no orange stigmas.

217

I have purchased "saffron seed" three times from different sources and all turned out to be safflower (*Carthamus tinctorius*) or "false saffron." Safflower is a tall, orange thistle that is used as one of the most common saffron adulterants; it is sometimes called "poor man's saffron." It is wise to start your saffron bed with bulbs.

## How To Use It

Because of its enormous value, saffron has been prey to all manner of adulterants, a crime punished by death in some past cultures. Grow your own and be sure it's pure.

Saffron has many medicinal virtues and is used as a dye herb, but it is primarily used for cooking. To release the full personality of the herb, crush the dried saffron threads and add them to two tablespoons hot water, enough to cover and reconstitute the threads. Use saffron sparingly; one-fourth teaspoon of the herb is usually sufficient for Scandinavian breads, English cakes, Pennsylvania Dutch potpie, Spanish paella, Italian risotto, a Louisiana fisherman's bouillabaisse, and Indian curry, or African couscous. Too much saffron can be overpowering, almost medicinal.

### *Mother Reppert's Schwenkfelder Saffron Bread*

| | |
|---|---|
| 1/4 | teaspoon saffron |
| 2 | tablespoons sugar |
| 1 | egg |
| 8 | cups flour |
| 1 | teaspoon salt |
| 1/3 | cup shortening, melted |
| 1 | package yeast |
| 1 | cup warm water |
| 1 | cup milk |
| 1/2 | cup raisins or currants |

1        egg, beaten
Sugar
1/4      cup almonds, c h o p p e d
         (optional)

Dissolve the saffron in hot water as explained.above. Mix the saffron, sugar, egg, flour, and salt. Add the melted shortening. Dissolve the yeast in 1 cup of warm water. Gradually add the yeast mixture, milk, and raisins to the dough, kneading as you go. Set the dough aside in a warm place, covered, until it doubles in size. Knead again. Shape into loaf or wreath. Leave loaf on greased tin to rise for 1 hour. Brush with egg, and sprinkle with sugar and chopped almonds (or a crumb mixture made of 2 cups brown sugar, 2 cups flour, 1 cup shortening, 2 teaspoons cinnamon, and 1/8 teaspoon crumbled saffron). Bake for 45 minutes at 325° F.

*Note*: The Schwenkfelders were the followers of Kaspar Schwenkfeld, a Silesian nobleman and Protestant reformer. They emigrated to America, landing at Philadelphia in 1734 and settling in southeastern Pennsylvania, where they found the religious freedom they sought. They brought saffron bulbs to their new home.

# Sage

| | |
|---|---|
| **Garden Sage** | Perennial, 2 to 3 feet |
| *(Salvia officinalis)* | |
| **Tricolor Sage** | Perennial, 1 foot |
| *(Salvia officinalis var. 'Tricolor')* | |
| **Golden Sage** | Perennial, 2 feet |
| *(Salvia officinalis var. 'Aurea')* | |
| **Purple Sage** | Perennial, 2 feet |
| *(Salvia officinalis var. 'Purpurascens')* | |
| **Pineapple Sage** | Tender perennial, 3 feet |
| *(Salvia elegans)* | |

## How to Grow It

"The herb of longevity" is a hardy semishrub that can be grown easily from seeds or cuttings. The gray-leaved *Salvia officinalis* is the most commonly grown, but many varieties make handsome contrasts in the herb garden. We also grow a sport of common gray garden sage, which is suitable for the smaller garden because of its compact form and small leaves.

Another unusual sage, always a favorite, is pineapple sage. Endowed with a strong pineapple scent and very fruity, this sage is a handsome garden plant. Unless an early frost nips the buds, pineapple sage ends the growing season with slender spikes of brilliant red flowers. Pineapple sage is a tender perennial, which must be wintered indoors. Dig it in August, transfer it to a tub, and bring it inside if a frost threatens. The leaves flavor fruit salads, iced tea, wine drinks, and herb butters. Whether or not you bring the whole plant indoors, be sure to take cuttings which are quickly rooted and wintered over on a sunny windowsill. The sturdy young plants can be planted outdoors in spring.

Sage is another easily grown herb. Once it is planted, you will have it for years. One plant is sufficient for the needs of the average family. Although we have lost some of the hybrids—they seem to come and go at will—our first plant of *officinalis* has been with us for more than fifteen years. Cut your sage back very early in spring if you do not wish it to exceed its allotted space. It may be cut and harvested at any time thereafter. We usually shear our sage right after it blooms in June. The lavender-blue spikes are lovely in the garden, in bouquets, and in herb wreaths.

Seeds may be planted outdoors early in spring or started inside in February. The seeds are fairly large and easily handled. Cuttings of new growth can be taken at any time from June through fall. With the aid of a rooting hormone and a shady bed of friable loam mixed with sand, the cuttings root readily, and taking cuttings is the only sure method of reproducing the colorful hybrids. We find that sage is a difficult houseplant.

## How To Use It

Because of its dominant flavor, sage is used to season bland meats, such as poultry, pork, or veal. Eels are traditionally wrapped in fresh sage leaves before cooking. Less than a teaspoon of dry sage will season the stuffing for a fifteen-pound turkey. Also try sage on squash, eggplant, or red beets, and sage-flavored cheese is great, especially in hot-cheese dishes. Simply add finely chopped sage, preferably fresh from the garden, with minced onion and coarsely ground black pepper, to grated cheese or cottage cheese. This recipe is delicious on crackers and as stuffing for celery.

One thing is sure—fresh sage is distinctly different from the dried form. Do try it fresh for a change of flavor. Add several fresh sage leaves, finely snipped, to one-quarter pound softened butter. Allow the butter to stand at least twenty-four hours before serving. Sage butter is pleasing on hot toast or biscuits. People who ordinarily cannot tolerate the flavor of sage find fresh sage butter surprisingly tasty and rarely recognize the flavor.

If not brewed for too long, sage tea is not at all an unpleasant drink. It is especially good combined with mint, with an added slice of lemon and honey for sweetness. It is recommended mainly for "its beneficial influence on the digestion" or if one feel a cold coming on.

On the island of Crete, sage tea is almost a national drink, obtainable at all times of the day in every restaurant or cafe. It has been noted in areas where sage tea is popular that the people are long-lived.

A strong sage tea, boiled in a black iron kettle, makes an old-fashioned rinse for dark hair. Rinse it through your hair as you bend over a basin; then, using a hairbrush, work the sage tea back into the hair. Aunt Bertha went to her grave at the age of eighty with coal-black hair, and now I've told her secret.

The botanical name for sage is *Salvia*, taken from the latin, meaning "to save." It refers to sage's ancient reputation for preserving good health. In centuries past, sage was more valuable as a medicine than as a culinary seasoning. Obviously, sage can be used for more than turkey dressing!

### *Tranquilla Tea*

| 1/2 | cup peppermint leaves (digestive) |
|---|---|
| 1 | tablespoon rosemary (sedative) |
| 1 | tablespoon sage (tonic) |

Mix the dried herbs together and store in a tea canister. Use 1 teaspoon of the herbs to 1 cup boiling water; steep 5 to 10 minutes, or until desired strength is achieved. Serve with honey.

### *Sage Butter For Pasta*

| 1/4 | pound butter |
|---|---|
| 2 to 4 | fresh sage leaves |
| 1 | clove garlic, minced |
| Salt to taste | |

Melt the butter in a skillet; add the chopped, fresh sage leaves and garlic; sauté until the sage has imparted its rich flavor to the butter. Pour over hot, cooked pasta and serve. Be prepared to honor requests for seconds.

223

# Santolina

| | |
|---|---|
| **Santolina (or Lavender Cotton)**<br>*(Santolina chamaecyparissus)* | Perennial, 3 feet |
| **Dwarf Santolina**<br>*(Santolina incana nana)* | Perennial, 8 inches |
| **Green Santolina**<br>*(Santolina virens)* | Perennial, 1 foot |
| **Gray Santolina**<br>*(Santolina neapolitana)* | Perennial, 1 foot |

Gray Santolina

## How To Grow It

Santolina is undoubtedly one of the most attractive plants in the herb garden. Its soft, gray mounds cry for recognition. All forms are striking ornamentals in any garden, but they are especially useful in establishing a pattern in the herb garden. They are most agreeable to clipping and, when planted closely, make neat hedges or knots. The silvery color is always best in full sun. Green santolina is a brilliant chartreuse; *neapolitana* has feathery, gray leaves and a pendulous effect; *incana nana* is a true miniature.

Bright yellow button flowers appear on santolina in July. Pick them for herb bouquets or dry them to use in winter arrangements. Occasionally they set seeds which can be germinated indoors to start new plants. We prefer propagating santolinas from cuttings taken in early spring or late summer. Side shoots sometimes layer themselves and can be removed to be planted elsewhere.

Where santolina is used as an edging or in knot gardens, clip it back severely in spring. An occasional shaping thereafter is all that's necessary to keep santolina attractively within bounds.

## How To Use It

Santolina is so decorative in the garden, it hardly needs to be more useful. Pick it to enhance any herbal bouquet; dry santolina to make herb wreaths; press the delicate, ferny leaves for pressed-flower pictures. Because its pungency is repellent to insects, santolina is useful in moth mixtures and vegetable garden sprays. Hang bunches in closets or lay dried sprigs between woolens in drawers as fragrant moth chasers.

Santolina forms dense growth on a woody trunk in only a few years, and is a natural for bonsai, the Japanese art of dwarfing plants in small containers, which is so popular today in America. Winter over santolina, thus grown, in a deep cold frame.

### *Favorite Moth Mixture*

| | |
|---|---|
| 2 | cups santolina |
| 2 | cups sandlewood |
| 2 | cups lemon verbena |
| 2 | cups lavender |
| 2 | cups patchouli leaves |
| 2 | cups rosemary |

Mix all ingredients (dried) together and place them in a tightly-lidded tin. Stir occasionally while they are aging for several weeks. Place mixture in flat cotton bags and use between woolens.

# Sassafras
*(Sassafras albidum)*

Perennial tree, 20 feet

## How To grow It

A tree of the wild, sassafras should be planted only in the background garden or, better yet, in the hedgerow. Sassafras is not easy to domesticate. It proliferates at a great rate, sending out many roots to be dug. It is not for the small garden.

Rarely reaching thirty feet, usually shrubby, sassafras has three kinds of typical leaves and greenish-yellow flowers that appear before the leaves in early spring. Where sassafras grows naturally, it is almost a "weed tree" and hard to eradicate. Don't hesitate to dig your own roots, all you want.

One of the many important herbs of the colonial period, sassafras opened trade with European countries, where people went wild over the remarkable new drink from the New World, made form the herb. "Sassafras, called by the inhabitants *winauk*, a kind of wood most pleasant and sweete smel, and of most rare vertues in physick for the cure of many disease," stated Thomas Hariot in a report on Virginia, dated 1590.

## How To Use It

The new drink of "pleasant and sweete smel" was hawked in the streets of London and, before that, in Spain, where it was used as an insect repellent. Sassafras has many "rare vertues."

Gather sassafras in spring when the ground has thawed sufficiently. Scrub the roots, shave them into small pieces, and dry and store them for later use. Whole pieces can be stored in drawers with woolens to repel moths.

Sassafras is America's oldest beverage—an Indian tonic, delicious and refreshing, hot or iced. Use 1/2 cup sassafras root bark to 4 cups water and boil for five to fifteen minutes, or until you have a good red color and good flavor. Sweeten with sugar or honey, and add cream or lemon, mint or spices.

If dried thoroughly between boilings, sassafras bark may be reused three to four times before all the flavor is extracted. A strong infusion can be kept if refrigerated (or warm on the back of the stove, as was frequently done in settlers' cabins). Dilute with hot water to serve.

The leaves also make a mild green tea, delicately flavored and fun for children to prepare when at camp, where sassafras grows.

## Iced Spiced Sassafras Tea

| | |
|---|---|
| 1 | ounce sassafras root bark |
| 1 | gallon water |
| 6 | cinnamon sticks |
| 24 | whole cloves |
| 2 | cups sugar |

Boil the bark in the water until a beautiful red tea is obtained; taste it occasionally until it has achieved the desired strength. Remove from heat; strain. Add the spices and sugar, and allow to cool. Serve over ice. This drink is refreshing on a hot summer's day. To store, remove the spices.

## Apple Butter
### (Lotwaerrick)

Here's a choice recipe for your collection, from my friends the Wieands of Lehigh County. This apple butter was sold, spread with cream cheese on homemade bread, at a local amusement park. People lined up for blocks to be served this Pennsylvania Dutch treat. The name Lotwaerrick means "a lot of work" in the dialect but is well worth the time and effort.

| | |
|---|---|
| 8 | cups quartered apples |
| 1 | quart cider |
| 1 | quart water |
| 10 | cups sugar |
| 2 | teaspoons cinnamon |
| 1/2 | teaspoon allspice |
| 1/2 | teaspoon cloves |
| 12-inch root sassafras, cut into small pieces | |

Combine apples, cider, and water, and cook until the apples are soft. Press through a strainer. Put the applesauce into a large, enameled roast pan and mix in 5 cups of the sugar. Bake in a 350° F. oven, stirring every half hour with a wooden spoon. After an hour, add the remaining sugar and spices. Cook 2 more hours, add the sassafras root. Cook another hour until thick and dark reddish-brown. Pour into sterilized jars and seal. Makes 5 quarts.

## Savory, Summer
*(Satureja hortensis)*
## Savory, Winter
*(Satureja montana)*

Annual, 1 foot

Perennial, 1 foot

Winter Savory

## How To Grow It

Annual or perennial, the savories can be used interchangeably. The more tender summer savory is known as *Bohnenkraut,* or the bean herb. It will do wonders for bean cookery and is also companionable with beans in the vegetable garden.

Grow summer savory from seeds, planting outdoors in May or indoors in March. It will thrive on a sunny windowsill. Easily transplanted, savory grows quickly to yield several harvests in a season. If you have poor germination, the tops of summer savory root quickly in damp vermiculite, giving you two plants where before you had only one.

Winter savory is a strong perennial, best grown from cuttings. If you pull shoots off the side of the plant, down close to the roots, you will have good, strong, well-started cuttings to plant. Winter savory is useful as an edging plant; at the edge of the garden its shrubby growth can be kept neatly clipped. Given full sun and moderately good soil, winter savory will reward you with tasty leaves all year.

# How To Use It

Never cook or serve beans—baked, kidney, buttered green, lima—without savory. Also add it to soup. Savory enhances beans and your reputation as a cook.

"When in doubt, use savory" is a good cook's motto, for stews and soups, with fish and meats, in salads, and any way you want to. Use more of the summer, less of the winter; more of the fresh, less of the dried. Savory is a most amenable herb.

Culpeper can hardly say enough for savory as medicine, recommending it for women's troubles, colic, the chest and lungs, for deafness, as a poultice for sciatica, "expelling wind," to clear "cold humours from the brain," and to revive dull spirits.

Planted as hedging or knots in the garden, winter savory is almost evergreen, and elegant when clipped. It is also considered a bee plant and, paradoxically, a remedy for bee stings. In the bee garden, allow savory to grow unrestrained so it flowers all summer.

## *Savory Green Beans*

| | |
|---|---|
| 1 | pound string beans |
| 1 | quart water |
| 1 | teaspoon dried savory (1 tablespoon fresh) |
| 3 | tablespoons butter |

Prepare the beans in your favorite way, cut long or short, and boil them just until tender. Add salt if desired. Drain the beans, and toss them in butter with savory.

# Scented Geraniums

## Rose Geranium
*(Pelargonium graveolens)*

Tender perennial, 3 feet

## Peppermint Geranium
*(Pelargonium tomentosum)*

Tender perennial, 2 feet

## Lemon Geranium
*(Pelargonium lemonium)*

Tender perennial, 1 foot

## How to Grow It

Fragrance is the built-in appeal of these easy, carefree, old-fashioned houseplants that compel admiration, and is reason enough to grow them. Collecting scented geraniums in all their varieties is a splendid hobby.

A sunny windowsill is the number one requirement for growing these Victorian charmers. Occasional watering, cool temperatures, humidity, and light feeding will ensure success.

Scented geraniums are amazingly easy to grow and soon reward a modicum of care with sizable growths. In fact, these are the easiest herbs to grow indoors.

Although a sunny window is one of the most important considerations, I have had a good response from scented geraniums grown under fluorescent lights, using bulbs especially designed to simulate sunshine. The lights are set eighteen inches above the potted plants, which are placed on trays of damp vermiculite, kept moist to provide humidity. The lighted plants shine like jewels in a dark, back corner of the room. They make a fragrant decoration.

Plant scented geraniums outside in summer, where they will grow to enormous proportions. Cut back the tops and roots before repotting the plants to return them to indoor living in the fall. They will rest a while before setting forth new growth.

To start new plants, firmly entrench in damp sand, six-inch cuttings, whose new growth has begun to mature, late in spring.

Cover with glass or plastic to trap moisture, and keep the plants in a north light. New growth will indicate that rooting has taken place.

Occasionally, seeds are available on the market for *Pelargonium odoratissimum*, an apple-scented geranium. A crown plant with dark, rounded leaves and intense fragrance, this geranium is very easy to grow and one of my favorites. Sometimes it self sows.

Hardy to 28° and in Southern gardens, these easy-care houseplants and herbs are endowed with many unique leaf patterns, providing form and color variation in any garden, inside and out.

## How To Use It

The main reason for growing scented geraniums (and their true charm) lies in their fascinating fragrance. Each kind has its own personality—orange, ginger, apricot, apple, nutmeg, rose, peppermint, lime, spice, and countless others. They are "mimic" plants, whose leaves release their aroma at a touch to perfume a room. They are also edible.

A leaf of the lemon-scented geranium will effectively flavor any cup of tea. Rose geranium leaves are traditionally used to flavor apple jelly or to line a pan of ordinary white cake. While the cake bakes, your kitchen will smell heavenly; after it cools, remove the leaves and dust the cake with rose geranium sugar

Velvety peppermint geranium can also be used to flavor sugar and beverages. Add a leaf to hot or cold drinks, for flavoring or as a garnish.

Steep a handful of the sweet-scented geranium leaves in a quart of boiling water, strain, and add to hot bath water. Gather all the dried leaves available to add to your potpourri, where they contribute fragrant bulk. I like any of them as a garnish for fruit bowls. Also, dainty, miniature nutmeg leaf may be placed on a pat of butter; the lemony ones are used in finger bowls.

Scented geraniums were prized during the Victorian era as valentines. These aromatic houseplants could be picked to send a sentimental message. To send your own valentine, gather the leaves in a little bunch, collar with a lace doily, and add ribbons and a card.

Here are messages to borrow from *The Language of Flowers*, an alphabet of floral emblems published in London in 1875.

| | |
|---|---|
| Geranium | Gentility |
| Apple Geranium | Present preference |
| Ivy Geranium | I engage you for the next dance. |
| Nutmeg Geranium | An expected meeting |
| Oakleaf Geranium | Lady, deign to smile |
| Scarlet Geranium | Comforting |
| Rose Geranium | Preference |
| Silver-leaved Geranium | Recall |

### Rose Geranium Sugar

4        leaves of rose geranium
2        cups sugar
A few drops red food coloring

Place all ingredients in the blender and blend on high speed for several minutes. Dry the sugar on a cookie sheet overnight before packaging it in jars. This aromatic pink sugar is delightful on the tea tray and attractive on sugar cookies. Vary this recipe by using peppermint geranium leaves and green coloring or lemon geranium leaves and yellow coloring.

### Rose Geranium Apple Jelly

Cut and core washed apples; cover with water and boil until soft enough to extract juice. Strain and add an amount of sugar equal to the amount of juice. Return to heat and stir until sugar dissolves. Add half a dozen rose geranium leaves and boil vigorously for 2 minutes. Remove from heat. Add a few drops of red food coloring, if desired. Skim the top; turn the jelly into fancy glasses, and replace cooked leaves with a fresh rose geranium leaf in each glass. Cover with paraffin.

## Sorrel, Garden (French)
*(Rumex scutatus)*

Perennial, 2 feet or more

### How To Grow It

Sorrel's arrow-shaped leaves thrust through the ground very early in spring. In years gone by they were a welcome change to a winter's diet of salted meats and dried vegetables. The crisp, succulent greens were brought here by early colonists because of their considerable role in daily fare. Today, elegant French restaurants eagerly seek these greens in the marketplace.

A strong, vigorously growing plant, sorrel is a perennial feature in the herb garden. Although it can be grown from seed, a quicker crop is possible from root division of an established plant. Large plants can be divided by thrusting a spade into the center of the clump and removing half to produce young, hearty plants. Do this as soon as possible in spring and no harm will befall the mother plant.

Once sorrel is planted, you can count on a ready crop of it every year beginning as early as March. It is easy to grow in a sunny, well-drained location. Cut back flowering stalks to keep it succulent and attractive.

Sorrel is closely related to the little weed called sour grass, and also to dock, both of which are edible if you prefer gathering foods in the wild.

## How To Use It

The succulent, light green leaves are very crisp and juicy. Gather them for tart additions to soup, salads, or vegetables. They can be frozen or dried for use in winter.

Wash the leaves carefully in several waters and add them to tossed green salads. Braise them in butter for a hot vegetable. A gourmet cook confided to me once that sorrel was the secret ingredient in the famous Senate Bean Soup. You will find many recipes using sorrel in French cookbooks.

Sorrel has a high acid content, which is perhaps why it is so good in early spring cookery. Certainly it is the oxalic acid that neutralizes the effect of stinging nettles when sorrel is rubbed directly on the affected skin. Also, acid probably was the reason our colonial housewife relished sorrel as an aid in cooking tough cuts of meat. Broiled or roasted while wrapped in large sorrel leaves, the meat was naturally tenderized. Another early American recipe for sorrel is described as an amazing "green sauce of sorrel and green gooseberries to serve with green goose." Green goose?

Sorrel and soup are synonymous. Here is my favorite spring soup, a lengthy old recipe considerably shortened by modern equipment and ingredients.

### *Quick And Easy Sorrel Soup*

| | |
|---|---|
| 1 | sizable handful of sorrel, midribs removed |
| 6 | leeks or onions |
| 4 | tablespoons chives |
| 2 | cloves garlic |

Blend above until almost pureed.

235

| 1/4 | pound butter |
| 6 | bouillon cubes |
| 8 | cups water |
| 1 | cup instant mashed potatoes (or 6 potatoes, cubed) |
| Salt to taste | |
| 1/4 | teaspoon rosemary (or 1 fresh tip) |
| 1 | teaspoon thyme |

Cook the blended herbs in the butter until limp, not brown; add the bouillon, water, and potatoes; cover and cook 30 minutes, adding more water if necessary. Reduce heat and add rosemary and thyme. Cook 5 minutes longer. Taste and, if necessary, correct the seasoning. Then add:

| 1 | can cream of chicken soup |
| 1 | can cream of mushroom soup |
| 1 | can evaporated milk |

Bring to a simmer; do not boil. Serve garnished with chopped chives, parsley, or chervil and paprika.

# Sweet Woodruff
## *(Galium odoratum)*

Perennial, 8 to 10 inches

## How To Grow It

This pretty ground cover grows rampantly in shaded areas, such as woods and hedgerows; in fact it demands shade. The leaves rise in attractive whorls along fragile stems and are especially appealing amidst fallen pine needles. Modest and unassuming, woodruff is one of the few plants willing to grow under pine trees.

Blooming in May, the bed comes alive with tiny, white, star-like flowers. To create a ground cover, plant small divisions of a clump of woodruff ten inches apart. Every little piece will grow, quickly filling in enough to blanket an area. Woodruff can also be grown from seeds.

Woodruff is an endearing small plant that grows wild in central Europe. Undoubtedly, it was brought here by German settlers who missed the *Waldmeister*. Translated as "master of the woods," the German nickname tells you how much they thought of little sweet woodruff.

## How To Use It

Curiously enough, *Waldmeister* is not particularly fragrant until it is dried, when it becomes overpowering with sweetness. Gather it in May when it is in flower and dry it for twenty minutes in a 150° F. oven. Step back when you open the oven door, for the fragrance will overwhelm you, perfuming the entire house. Store the dried herb in large, dark jars for later use.

In centuries past, *Waldmeister's* sweetness was enjoyed in mattresses and in fragrant pillows. It was also used as a strewing herb to repel insects. By all means, include all the woodruff you wish in your potpourris, to which the bright green, vanilla-scented leaves add color and fragrance as well as acting as a homegrown fixative.

A relaxing tea may be made by steeping one teaspoon of the herb to a cup of boiling water. Said to relieve headaches and to have a calming effect, woodruff tea is recommended as a nightcap.

Traditionally, sweet woodruff is used to prepare *mailbowle*, a delicious wine. Add sprigs of dried sweet woodruff to you favorite dry white wine. Allow it to steep for several hours before serving. Undiluted apple juice may be substituted for wine. Steeped overnight, it has a surprisingly exhilarating effect and always makes a tremendous hit wherever it is served.

A good hostess will serve both these punches, alcoholic and non-alcoholic, with great confidence.

### Sweet Woodruff Punch

Steep 1/2 cup green-dried woodruff in a small amount of apple juice overnight. Strain and add the remainder of a 46-ounce can of apple juice and a quart of ginger ale. Pour over a small box of frozen sliced strawberries. Sweeten with 1/2 cup sugar mashed together with a sliced lemon, rind and all. Garnish by floating sliced strawberries and woodruff in the punch bowl. This recipe serves 12 and may be doubled or tripled.

### May Bowl

| | |
|---|---|
| 1 | cup dried woodruff |
| 1 | bottle dry white wine |
| 1 | bottle champagne |

| 1 | bottle club soda |
| --- | --- |
| Fresh strawberries, sliced | |
| 1 | orange, sliced |
| Violet flowers | |
| Sprigs of fresh sweet woodruff | |

Steep the dried woodruff in the white wine overnight. Strain through muslin and pour over ice in a large punch bowl. Add champagne and club soda to taste; garnish with the fruit and herbs and serve it forth.

*Sweet Woodruff*

# Tansy
*(Tanacetum vulgare)*
# Tansy, Fern Leaf
*(Tanacetum vulgare var. crispum)*

Perennial, 3 feet

Perennial, 2 feet

## How To Grow It

A tall herb, suitable only for the large garden, or as a background plant or tucked among the shrubbery, tansy has long escaped the early settler's garden and made itself at home in open, sunny fields, meadows and picturesque roadsides. Now "hereditary in the new land," tansy is looked upon as sometimes weed, sometimes wildflower, and always herb. It grows from New York to California, wherever the soil and climate suit it.

Tansy can be grown from its very fine seed planted early in spring or from root divisions taken from established plants before mid-May. By June, tansy is very tall, and the stalks cannot be divided successfully. The roots are adventurous, always seeking new territory and invading surrounding clumps of herbs. All this endless yardage of roots needs to be dug and removed, whether or not you intend to enlarge your tansy patch with the root divisions.

*Crispum* has more elegantly curled leaves and is not nearly so rampant a grower. It is an asset to any perennial border.

# How To Use It

Golden buttons in broad, terminal clusters appear in midsummer. Pick and enjoy them in big bouquets along with black-eyed Susans, goldenrod, and yarrow, all gloriously in bloom at the same time. This bouquet will dry naturally and last through winter, with the tansy buttons turning a rich dark brown.

Tansy tea was once taken for gout, colic, rheumatism, arthritis, colds, and almost anything else, including the plague. This tea is incredibly bitter. Because it was one of the first herbs to appear in the garden, those early fresh greens were welcomed as a spring tonic. Tansy was also prepared with many eggs in a "tansy pudding," an acquired taste, I'm sure.

Since the Middle Ages, tansy has been respected as a medicinal tea and insect repellent. Of these uses, the most valid use today is a safe, nonpoisonous ant repellent made from tansy. It works. Place the fresh leaves wherever ants are a problem. Sew little bags for the dried leaves and lay them on your shelves; or boil an infusion of tansy in water to pour over really bad invasions. That's how we successfully cleared ants from a flagstone patio. Now we understand tansy's value as an ancient strewing herb.

## Herbal Plant Spray

Equal parts tansy, wormwood and rue, fresh from the garden (or dried) are boiled in a quart of water for 5-10 minutes. Strain into a large sprinkling can, fill with water, and apply. Safe, effective, and organic, it can be used on food crops as well as houseplants as often as necessary to control aphids, whitefly, and red spider.

# Tarragon
*(Artemisia dracunculus var. sativa)*

Perennial, 1 1/2 feet

## How to Grow It

Be not deceived by tarragon seeds. They will produce a tall, rank-growing variety utterly worthless as a seasoning. Avoid tarragon seeds or the plants of tarragon grown from seed. They will take over your garden without producing one useful leaf.

To grow tarragon, one must begin with a plant of the true culinary variety, usually referred to as "French." It is propagated by root divisions or cutting only.

Lift the plant in early spring and divide it into as many rooted pieces as possible; then replant. After growth begins, the tops can be cut back and rooted with the aid of rooting hormone and damp sand. Keep them moist in a shaded corner of the garden. Be sure to remove the lower leaves on each cutting and insert the cuttings firmly in the rooting medium. After they have rooted, plant the young tarragons in a border with good soil and good drainage, where they will receive at least half a day of sun.

Surplus plants can be potted as winter houseplants. Like all herbaceous perennials however, tarragon responds to the seasons and will need a rest period. At some time during the winter months, put it outside and let it go dormant. After you bring tarragon back into the warmth, water it, and in a month or so new shoots will spring from below the soil line as its life cycle continues. Cut back any dried-off tops, for they'll not sprout again.

## How To Use It

Tarragon is the prettiest in spring when it grows with amazing rapidity. Cut the plants as soon as they are a foot high. Do this several times during the growing season, and you'll have thrifty, compact tarragon plants, as well as a generous harvest.

If you've never tasted fresh tarragon, you are in for quite a treat. There is almost no relationship between fresh and dried tarragon.

Dry your harvest out of the sun, and carefully pick the leaves off the stems, retaining the whole leaf wherever possible. Therein lies our secret of success with dried tarragon. Crush the leaf when you use it to release the anise-like flavor.

Tarragon was said to be good for the bite of "little dragons." We aren't bothered much by dragons, big or little, so we use it, instead, as a superb seasoning for chicken, salads, eggs, fish (especially lobster), tomatoes, sauces, lamb, and meat marinades. Its versatility in cookery is unequaled.

Tarragon can be frozen and kept in a tight container, but the essence is best caught and preserved in vinegar. Use your harvest while it's fresh; freeze or dry some for later; and be absolutely sure to make at least a gallon of tarragon vinegar. Make two gallons if you are on a charity bazaar committee, for it sells well.

### *Tarragon Vinegar*

| | |
|---|---|
| 2 | quarts tarragon tips |
| 4 | cloves garlic (optional) |
| 1 | gallon apple cider vinegar |

243

Wash and pick over the tarragon; cram it into a large jar or crock. Pour the hot, not boiling, vinegar over the tarragon. Allow it to stand in the sun for 2 weeks; stir or shake daily. Strain and bottle for later use. If too strong, this vinegar can be diluted. Use it on salads and in sauces.

Tarragon

# Thyme

| | |
|---|---|
| **Creeping Thyme** | Perennial, 3 inches |
| *(Thymus serphyllum)* | |
| **Culinary Thyme** | Perennial, 1 foot or less |
| *(Thymus vulgaris)* | |
| **Lemon Thyme** | Perennial, 1 foot |
| *(Thymus citriodorus)* | |
| **Caraway Thyme** | Perennial, 4 inches |
| *(Thymus herba-barona)* | |

## How To Grow It

There are many varieties of thyme—golden-leaved, silver-edged, wooly, lemon-scented, flowered in white, lavender, pink, and red. The two main categories are upright and creeping. All are edible, although most varieties grown for culinary purposes are upright.

The creeping thymes (sometimes called Mother-of-thyme) make excellent ground covers, especially between the cracks of flagstone. It is said that "the more it is trodden upon the faster it grows." Thyme is a divinely fragrant outdoor carpet if the soil, moisture, drainage, and exposure are right.

The culinary thymes are small, shrubby upright plants which are superb as an edging in the herb garden or as accent plants in the rock garden. They are woody-stemmed, hardy, and flowering. A healthy thyme plant by the kitchen door will provide her snippets during most months of the year, even when covered by snow. Fresh from the garden is best, of course, but thyme can be harvested, bunched, hung, dried, and stored in your spice rack. A sprig of fresh thyme is equal to a quarter teaspoon of the dried.

Propagating thyme is easy if you know the secret. Take very small cuttings, only three inches to five inches long, preferably unbranched and with a "heel" of the old stem. Dab each cutting in rooting powder and press it into good, receptive earth. Now cover the rooting end with a small rock. This acts as a perfect mulch, retaining necessary moisture while marking the spot so the little cutting is not lost. The cutting will take off on its own in no time and be a proper thyme plant.

Thyme (pronounced "*time*") is an ancient herb symbolic of innocence and courage. Centuries ago young maidens wore thyme in their hair as a sign they were available for marriage—in my opinion, a rare combination of innocence and courage. Once married, I'm sure they quickly discovered thyme's culinary virtues. Thyme is also a desirable addition to fragrant mixtures.


## How To Use It

Best known as a culinary herb, thyme is useful blended with cheese, vegetable juices, fish (especially clam chowder), beef, other meats, poultry, and vegetables. A tea of thyme, made by steeping one teaspoon of the dried herb to a cup of boiling water for about five minutes, is a palatable hot beverage, recommended to quell a hangover.

'Tis said of thyme, a bee herb, that "it yielded most and best honie." The oil, extracted commercially, is used as a powerful antiseptic, in cough medicines, as an insect repellent, and one of the ancient strewing herbs. Thyme has many virtues.

### *Thymed Hamburgers*

Make patties from ground round or your own favorite hamburger mixture. Sprinkle a pan liberally with thyme and salt; heat the herb to release its flavor. Fry the patties in the pan.

### Caraway Thyme Bread

1/4     pound butter, softened
2     tablespoons caraway thyme
        leaves, fresh or dried

Mix the butter and herb; spread on rye bread. Heat the bread under the broiler for a few minutes until bubbly.

### Holy Hay

This is reputed to have been used during Biblical days to stuff mattresses and to repel fleas and other stable insects. Perhaps it was the bedding used to line the manger at Bethlehem.

Gather and dry equal quantities of thyme, bedstraw, and pennyroyal and add the fragrant symbolic Holy Hay to the Christmas créche in your church or home.

### Mother-Of-Thyme Tea

"An infusion of it made and drank in the manner of tea is pleasant, and is an excellent remedy for headaches and giddiness.... It certainly cures that troublesome disease the nightmare. A gentleman afflicted terribly with that complaint took a strong infusion of it by way of remedy and was free from it many years. Afterwards the disorder returned, but always gave way to the same remedy."

*Nature the Best Physician,*
by Joseph Taylor, 1818

# Watercress
*(Nasturtium officinale)*

Perennial, low to 6 inches

## How To Grow It

Peppery native of Europe, watercress was brought here by the earliest settlers and has since escaped into streams all across the northern tier of America. A small, dark green-leaved plant, it enjoys shallow, clear, cold waters. Now a valuable commercial crop, watercress is shipped into the markets of all major cities. If you know where it grows, gather the pungent herb from the nearest stream.

Watercress can be grown from seeds germinated in ordinary soil then transplanted to the damp fringes of gently running waters, where it takes off, soon naturalizing itself in the stream. Because watercress loves water, cuttings of it will root readily in a tumbler on your windowsill. Buy a bunch of watercress in the nearest market, use half, and root the other half in water or damp sand. Change the water occasionally. Snip the cuttings as needed, or plant them in a suitably wet place. We have also had success growing watercress in a large, shallow pot kept constantly moist and in full sun.

## How To Use It

Watercress and its close cousin, nasturtium, may be used almost interchangeably. All parts of this delightful, popular herb are edible. It can be a zesty seasoning for sandwiches or salads and is an attractive, vitamin-rich, green garnish. A tasty tea can be made from the leaves, stems, and roots.

If you are blessed with an abundant supply of this favorite herb, cook it in butter or cream it like spinach. Puréed and creamed, watercress makes an unusual soup.

## *Watercress Sandwiches*

Lay sprigs of thoroughly washed watercress in the center of each slice of buttered, white bread with the crusts removed, and roll up. Serve with cress showing at both ends. Make with mayonnaise, if you wish. These sandwiches are a favorite for tea.

## Wormwood
*(Artemisia absinthium*

Perennial, 3 feet

### How To Grow It

The handsome, grayed foliage of wormwood is dazzling in full sun. Herb of the ancients, wormwood is easily grown but should be kept by itself in the garden because the bitterness washed off the leaves by the rain is said to affect other herbs. Fennel, caraway, anise, and sage definitely resent being close to wormwood, which inhibits their growth.

Wormwood may be grown from seeds, root divisions, or cuttings taken in June, and will occasionally self-sow if all the flowering tops have not been harvested. The seeds can be sown in fall or spring. To plant them in the fall, prepare a seedbed, pat in the seeds, and cover with a board. Remove the board in the spring, and you will have dozens of wormwood plants.

# How To Use It

As vermifuge, disinfectant, insect repellent, and aid to digestion, wormwood is powerful medicine, one of the bitterest. We gather every bit of wormwood the garden produces and put it to many uses.

The classic use of wormwood is in the green liqueur absinthe, which is considered addictive, dangerous, and is, therefore, outlawed in France and in vermouth. The flowers and leaves can be steeped in brandy for several weeks to make a homemade aid to digestion. Care should be taken not to use too much of this herb, since it has dangerous properties.

As a strewing herb, wormwood repels household vermin and was once believed to disinfect the air. An infusion of wormwood was an old home remedy known and used for any ailments. A bath of this infusion (1 teaspoon to a quart of water) repels fleas on cats and dogs. You may use the same solution to discourage slugs and beetles in the garden. When kitchen screens or counter tops are washed with this wormwood solution, flies will go elsewhere. Spray it on fruit trees or vegetables, and aphids will be repelled, but be sure to wash away any bitter residue before eating the sprayed foods.

Our favorite use of wormwood is to combine it with other grayed herbs, such as silver king, sage, santolina, and silver mint to make a base for herbal wreaths. Oh, the fragrance! We always work with the fresh herbs, allowing them to dry in position on the wreath frame. Bitter though it be, its fragrance is to be enjoyed.

## All-Purpose Wormwood Infusion

| | |
|---|---|
| 1 | quart boiling water |
| 1 | handful wormwood tops and flowers, fresh or dried |

Pour the water over the herb and steep until cold. Strain and bottle to use as a plant spray, pet wash, and disinfectant.

| | |
|---|---|
| **Yarrow, Common** | Perennial, 1 foot |
| *(Achillea millefolium)* | |
| **Yarrow, Pink** | Perennial, 2 feet |
| *Achillea millefolium, var 'Rosea')* | |
| **Yarrow, Golden** | Perennial, 3 feet |
| *(Achillea filipendulina)* | |

### How To Grow It

These hardy plants may be started from seeds or, more easily, from divisions taken from the roots of established plants early in spring. Yarrow must have full sun, an open area, and fairly good soil that is very well drained and kept free of weeds.

Common wild yarrow has a small, ferny leaf, white or pink flowers, and grows only a foot tall. The white form grows in fields, and the pink to red cultivars are more often found in gardens.

Golden plates of ornamental yarrow grace the summer garden. Yarrow is best grown as a tall, background plant, with a large area to call its own. The flowers are gathered shortly after they emerge, then dried for winter bouquets. No need to hang them—they will dry upright, in a tall vase with water placed out of the sun. Enjoy them in a bouquet while they are drying.

Many other varieties of yarrow are available for perennial borders, and low-growing varieties are excellent for the rockery. Most yarrows are invasive and need to be cut back early in spring.

### How To Use It

The white yarrow of the fields used to be sought during wars. Called "soldier's woundwort," its reputation for staunching the flow of blood goes back to Achilles, who, according to legend, used it on his heel; hence, its botanical name. An ointment for wounds was made by bruising the leaves and boiling them in lard.

Yarrow has been employed in many other medicinal concoctions—as tea for a cold, as a head wash for baldness, and as snuff. The flowers and leaves were used, both being pungently bitter. Today we enjoy them in bouquets of herbs.

### Yarrow Pillow Talk

I am fond of the old superstition that an ounce of yarrow in a little packet placed under your pillow will cause you to dream of your future spouse. You are to repeat the following charm:

> "Thou pretty herb of Venus tree,
> Thy true name it is Yarrow;
> Know who my bosom friend must be,
> Pray tell thou me to-morrow."

# BIBLIOGRAPHY

Angier, Bradford. *Field Guide to Edible Wild Plants.* Harrisburg: Stackpole Books, 1975.

Baker, Margaret. *Discovering the Folklore of Plants.* England: Shire Publications, 1969.

Balls, Edward K. *Early Uses of California Plants* . Los Angeles: University of California Press, 1972.

Bartram, Wm. *Travels of Wm. Bartram,* edited by Mark Van Doren. Original, 1792. New York: Dover Publications, 1928.

Beeton, Mrs. Isabella. *The Book of Household Management,* London, 1861. Reprint, New York: Farrar, Straus, and Giroux, 1968.

Beston, Henry. *Herbs and the Earth.* New York: Doubleday & Co., 1935.

Brown, Alice Cooke. *Early American Herb Recipes.* New York: Bonanza, 1966.

Brownlow, Margaret. *Herbs and the Fragrant Garden,* 2d ed. New York: McGraw-Hill Book Co., 1963.

Bullock, Mrs. Helen. *The Williamsburg Art of Cookery or Accomplish'd Gentlewoman's Companion.* Original, 1742. Reprint, Colonial Williamsburg, Va., 1966.

Bunyard, Edward A. *Old Garden Roses.* England: Country Lift, Ltd., 1936.

Campbell, Mary Mason. *Betty Crocker's Kitchen Gardens.* New York: Universal Publishing, Inc., 1971.

Clarkson, Rosetta E. *Herbs: Their Culture and Uses.* The Macmillan Company, 1942.

———. *Herbs and Savory Seeds* (1939). Reprint, New York: Dover Publications, 1972.

Coats, Peter. *Flowers in History.* New York: The Viking Press, Inc., 1970.

Collin, Mary A. *Everyday Cooking with Herbs.* Garden City, N.Y.: Doubleday & Co., 1974.

Cooke, Alistair. *America.* New York: Alfred A. Knopf, Inc., 1974.

Coon, Nelson. *Using Wayside Plants for Healing.* New York: Hearthside Press, Inc., 1962.

_____ *The Dictionary of Useful Plants.* Emmaus, Pa.: Rodale Press, 1974.

Culbreth, David M. R., M.D. *A Manual of Materia Medica and Pharmacology.* Philadelphia: Lea and Febiger, 1927.

Culpeper, Nicholas (1616-1654). *Culpeper's Complete Herbal: A Comprehensive Description of Nearly All Herbs with Their Medicinal Properties and Directions for Compounding the Medicines Extracted from Them.* Reprint, London: W. Foulsham & Co., Ltd.

Dutton, Joan Parry. *The Flower World of Williamsburg.* Colonial Williamsburg, Va., 1962.

Earle, Alice Morse. *Old Time Gardens.* New York: The Macmillan Company, 1901.

Fisher, Louise B. *An Eighteenth Century Garland* . Colonial Williamsburg, Va., 1951.

Fletcher, H. L. V. *Herbs.* England: Drake Publishers, 1972.

Foley, Daniel J., ed. *Herbs for Use and for Delight: An Anthology from The Herbalist.* A publication of The Herb Society of America. New York: Dover Publications, 1974.

Foster, Gertrude B. *Herbs for Every Garden.* New York: E. P. Dutton & Co., Inc. 1966.

Fox, Helen Morgenthau. *Gardening with Herbs for Flavor and Fragrance.* Reprint, New York: Dover Publications, 1970.

Freeman, Margaret B. *Herbs for the Mediaeval Household* . New York: The Metropolitan Museum of Art, 1971.

Gibbons, Euell. *Stalking the Healthful Herbs.* New York: David McKay Co., Inc., 1966.

Grieve, Mrs. M. *A Modern Herbal* . In 2 vols. London: Hafner Publishing, 1970

Hermann, Matthias. *Herbs and Medicinal Flowers.* New York: Galahad Books, 1973.

Humphries, Pat, and Reppert, Bertha. *Potpourri: Recipes and Crafts*, Mechanicsburg, Pa.: The Rosemary House, 1973.

Jaques, H. E. *Plants We Eat and Wear.* Published by the author. Iowa: Mt. Pleasant, 1943.

Jones, Dorothy Bovee. *The Herb Garden.* Philadelphia, Dorrance & Co., 1972.

Keays, Mrs. Frederick Love. *Old Roses.* New York: The Macmillan Company, 1935.

254

Kelsey, Harlan P., and Dayton, William A. *Standardized Plant Names* . U.S. Department of Agriculture for the American Joint Committee on Horticultural Nomenclature. Harrisburg, Pa.: J. Horace McFarland Co., 1942.

Koogle, J. D. *The Farmer's Own Book*. Baltimore: McCoull & Slater, 1857.

Krochmal, Connie. *A Guide to Natural Cosmetics* . New York: Quadrangle Press, 1973.

Lehner, Ernest and Johanna. *Folklore and Odysseys of Food and the Medicinal Plants*. New York: Tudor Publishing Co., 1962.

Leighton, Ann. *Early American Gardens "for Meate or Medicine."* Boston: Houghton Mifflin Co., 1970.

Levy, Juliette de Bairacli. *Herbal Handbook for Farm and Stable*. London: Faber and Faber Ltd., 1963.

Leyel, Mrs. C. F. *The Magic of Herbs*. London: Jonathan Cape, 1932.

Lust, John. *The Herb Book*. New York: Bantam Books, 1974.

McFarland, J. Horace. *Standardized Plant Names* . J. Horace McFarland Co. for the American Joint Committee on Horticultural Nomenclature. Harrisburg: Mt. Pleasant Press, 1942.

Meyer, Joseph E. *The Herbalist*. Original, 1918. Reprint, New York: Sterling Publishing Co., 1973.

Miloradovich, Milo. *The Art of Cooking with Herbs and Spices*. Garden City N.Y.: Doubleday & Co., 1950.

Montagne, Prosper. *Larousse Gastronomique, The Encyclopedia of Food, Wine & Cookery*. New York: Crown Publishers, Inc., 1961.

Petulengro, Gipsy. *Romany Remedies and Recipes*. Reprint, Hollywood: Newcastle Pushing, 1972.

Philbrick, Helen, and Gregg, Richard. *Companion Plants and How to Use Them*. Old Greenwich, Conn.: The Devin-Adair Company, 1974.

Phipps, Frances. *Colonial Kitchens, Their Furnishings, and Their Gardens*. New York: Hawthorn Books, 1972.

Pollock, Allan. *Botanical Index to All the Medicinal Plants, Barks, Roots, Seeds and Flowers Usually Kept by Druggists*. New York: Allan Pollock, 1874.

Rohde, Eleanour Sinclair. *A Garden of Herbs* (1939). Reprint, New York: Dover Publications, 1969.

. *The Old English Herbals* (1922). Reprint, New York: Dover Publications, 1971.

Rosengarten, Frederic, Jr. *The Book of Spices*. Philadelphia: Livingston Publishing Co., 1969.

Shaeffer, Elizabeth. *Dandelion, Pokeweed, and Goosefoot* . Reading, Mass.: Young Scott Books, 1972.

Simmons, Adelma Grenier. *The Illustrated Herbal Handbook*. New York: Hawthorn Books, 1972.

Smith, Bradley. *Spain: A History in Art* . New York: Simon and Schuster, 1966.

Stimpson, George. *A Book About a Thousand Things*. New York: Harper & Bros., 1946.

Taylor, Norman, ed. *The Garden Dictionary*. Boston and New York: Houghton Mifflin Co., 1936.

Taylor, Raymond L. *Plants of Colonial Days*. Williamsburg, Va.: Printed for Colonial Williamsburg by the Dietz Press, 1952.

Thomas, Graham Stuart. *The Old Shrub Roses*. Boston: Charles T. Branford Co., 1956.

Thomas, John J. *The American Fruit Culturist* . New York: William Wood and Co., 1885.

Webster, Helen Noyes. *Herbs: Hot to Grow Them and How to Use Them*. Boston: Charles T. Branford Co., 1959.

Wieand, Paul R. *Folk Medicine Plants Used in the Pennsylvania Dutch Country*. Wieand's Pennsylvania Dutch, 1961.

Willison, George F. *Saints and Strangers*. New York: Reynal & Hitchcock, 1945.

Wright, Richardson. *The Story of Gardening*. New York: Garden City Publishing, 1938.

U.S. Dept. of Agriculture. *Drug Plants Under Cultivation*. Farmers Bulletin No. 663, Washington, D.C.: Govt. Printing Office, 1915.

(author unknown) *All You Need to Know About Herbs*. A periodical. London: Marshall Cavendish Ltd., 1973.

‘_____. *Dye Plants and Dyeing, A Handbook*. New York: Brooklyn Botanic Gardens, 1965.

_____. The "Home Queen" World's Fair Souvenir Cook Book. Philadelphia: J. W. Keeler & Co., 1893.

# GENERAL INDEX

261

**SUGGESTED PLANS
FOR YOUR HERB
GARDEN ARE TO
BE FOUND ON
PAGES: X, 3, 4, 8, 9,
34, 88, 124, 186, 206**

# INDEX OF CRAFTS

# Ꜧerbs

Ꜧ little garden in which to walk,
an immensity in which to dream;
at one's feet that which can be
cultivated and plucked; overhead
that which one can study and
meditate upon; some herbs on
earth and all the stars in
the sky.

~ Hugo

265

# INDEX OF RECIPES

Hyssop

# AWARDS

## For Bertha Reppert's
## "Herbs With Confidence"

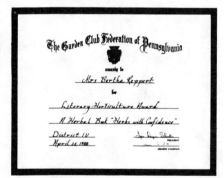

**HERBS WITH CONFIDENCE**

A primer published in 1986 that answers many questions asked at the Rosemary House. Includes 135 tried and true recipes, 55 herb crafts and 50 herbs -- lovingly written in depth.

*The Rosemary House, Inc.*
120 S. Market St.
Mechanicsburg, PA 17055

**The Helen S. Hull Plaque**
**for Literary Horticultural Interest**     **Pennsylvania**
**Herbs with Confidence by Bertha Reppert**
Herbs are the "workhorses of the plant kingdom" and their uses are again becoming a must for every gardener, cook, homemaker, and artistic designer. This literary endeavor is a book that is useful to all phases of plant use and to all persons using herbs. It is multi-faceted in its scope.

*'There's Rosemary, that's for Remembrance, I pray you love, remember...'*
*...Shakespeare*